A5
A Project Manager's Guide:
Delivering useful quality systems to time and budget

THE INFORMATION SYSTEMS GUIDES

MANAGEMENT AND PLANNING SET
A1   An Introduction to Information Systems in Government
A2   Strategic Planning for Information Systems
A3   Computer and Office Systems Planning
A4   Telecommunications Planning
A5   A Project Manager's Guide

SYSTEMS DEVELOPMENT SET
B1   The Users' Role in Systems Development
B2   The Feasibility Study
B3   The Full Study
B4   Appraising Investment in Information Systems
B5   The Operational Requirement
B6   Procurement
B7   Evaluation
B8   Systems Engineering

SERVICE MANAGEMENT SET
C1   Services Management
C2   Environmental Services
C3   Contingency Planning
C4   Security and Privacy
C5   Telecommunications Operation and Management
C6   Capacity Planning
C7   Availability Planning

OFFICE USERS' SET
D1   Small Systems
D2   Microcomputer Systems and Software
D3   Office System Facilities

INFORMATION SYSTEMS SERVICES INDUSTRY SET
E1   The Information Systems Services Industry
E2   The Hire and Management of Consultants
E3   Turnkey Projects
E4   Facilities Management

The Information Systems Guides

A5
A Project Manager's Guide:
Delivering useful quality systems to
time and budget

Ken Baldwin

John Wiley & Sons
Chichester ◇ New York ◇ Brisbane ◇ Toronto ◇ Singapore

Published by John Wiley and Sons Ltd, on behalf of:
HM Treasury,
Central Computer and Telecommunications Agency,
157-161 Millbank, London SW1P 4RT
Telephone 01 217-3331

For information about the availability of the
CCTA Information Systems Guides, contact:
John Wiley and Sons Ltd,
Baffins Lane, Chichester, PO19 1UD, UK.
Telephone 0243 779777

Technical editing and design by:
Praxis Systems plc, 20 Manvers Street, Bath BA1 1PX, UK.

British Library Cataloguing in Publication Data
A project manager's guide. - (CCTA information systems
  guides; A5).
  1. Computer systems
  I. Title   II. Central Computer and Telecommunications
  Agency   III. Series
  004

ISBN 0 471 92525 X

Printed in Great Britain at the Alden Press
Oxford London and Northampton

Contents

Preface

As the Minister responsible for the CCTA, I welcome the publication of this series of IS Guides.

Because of its experience throughout Government and elsewhere, CCTA is uniquely placed to provide advice and guidance on Information Systems. To pass on this information effectively requires a structured and comprehensive approach, focussing on the needs of Government departments, and their new executive agencies.

Existing CCTA guidance addresses a wide range of audiences, ranging from staff responsible at the technical level to the senior management of departments. These new Guides have two principal audiences: business managers and planners; and those whose job it is to develop and manage the Information Systems which support the business of Government.

The Guides are a major investment by CCTA. They seek to improve the awareness, knowledge and practices of Government departments and agencies on Information Systems. I believe they will increase senior management's awareness of the potential of Information Systems, and of the need to think about Information Systems and plan them strategically. They will improve the knowledge of those who are developing and managing Information Systems, by informing them about best practices and about the methods and standards to adopt. In short, the Guides are designed to give departments a better command of the recommended techniques and practices so that they can take their management decisions confidently.

I also hope that the IS Guides will give the private sector a valuable insight into Government expectations and approaches and assist in forging more beneficial links between the private and public sectors.

Above all, CCTA's Informations Systems Guides aim to help Government departments and agencies improve the effectiveness and quality of their Information Systems. I commend them to you.

Richard Ryder OBE MP
Economic Secretary

The Information Systems Guides

Exploiting Information Systems

The purpose of these guides is to enable managers to realise the potential of Information Systems. They are written for managers rather than technicians; they aim to provide enough material for informed decision-making, but not an excess of technical detail.

The guides are arranged in five sets. Each set expects a slightly different readership, but users of the guides may nevertheless find valuable information in a number of sets.

Planning Information Systems

The Planning and Management Set - the A set - is intended for those departmental managers who are concerned with the overall planning and management of Information Systems.

A1   An Introduction to Information Systems in Government: *Setting the scene*

A2   Strategic Planning for Information Systems: *Ensuring that the business benefits*

A3   Computer and Office Systems Planning: *Resourcing tactical plans*

A4   Telecommunications Planning: *Understanding the key issues*

A5   A Project Manager's Guide: *Delivering useful quality systems to time and budget*

Developing Information Systems

The Systems Development Set - the B set - is concerned with the processes which translate the plans into usable systems.

B1   The Users' Role in Systems Development: *Getting involved*

B2   The Feasibility Study: *Scoping the system*

B3   The Full Study: *Meeting the requirement*

B4   Appraising Investment in Information Systems: *Examining the options*

B5   The Operational Requirement: *Saying what you want*

B6   Procurement: *Getting what you want*

B7   Evaluation: *Choosing best value for money*

B8   Systems Engineering: *Designing and building quality systems*

Managing the provision of IS services

The Service Management Set - the C set - is intended for those involved in the provision of Information Systems services, and deals with topics of interest to IT Services managers and their staff, Operations managers, Network managers, Office Service managers, and IT Security personnel.

C1	Services Management: *Delivering quality service*
C2	Environmental Services: *Working comfortably*
C3	Contingency Planning: *Anticipating disaster*
C4	Security and Privacy: *Protecting information systems*
C5	Telecommunications Operation and Management: *Managing networks*
C6	Capacity Planning: *Anticipating the need*
C7	Availability Planning: *Improving reliability and resilience*

Using IS in the office

The Office User's Set - the D set - is aimed at those managers who need information to help them decide whether they should introduce local computerised methods to help in the work for which they are responsible.

D1	Small Systems: *Setting up local systems*
D2	Microcomputer Systems and Software: *Choosing and using micros*
D3	Office System Facilities: *Understanding what is available*

Buying consultancy and IS services

The IS Services Industry Set - the E set - contains guidance about the various IS services which are available from the private sector. Advice is given on how departments should manage and exploit external services.

E1	The Information Systems Services Industry: *Obtaining external services*
E2	The Hire and Management of Consultants: *Buying in advice and assistance*
E3	Turnkey Projects: *Contracting for the design and delivery of a complete information system*
E4	Facilities Management: *Contracting for the provision of information system services*

Part A   Setting the Project Management Scene

1   Introduction

1.1   Purpose of this guide

This guide is one of a series aimed at those who are planning, developing and implementing Information Systems. It describes the Project Manager's role and the techniques used in project management.

This guide is intended for middle-to-senior level managers who are about to manage a project in the information systems field. It assumes that you are an experienced manager having the usual management skills. However, you may have come from the domain of either the business user or the Information Technology (IT) provider, so it makes no assumptions about your background. The various points raised are indicated by marginal headings and are included in the index. So, as well as reading straight through the guide, you will be able to dip in to find guidance on the particular matter of concern as you approach that point in the life of the project.

You have been told that managing an IS project is somehow different from the sort of management that you have practised in the past. But is this necessarily so? Surely all the well known principles of management must still apply? Of course they do, **but** there are some differences, if only because project management invariably crosses organisational boundaries, and information systems have their risks as well as opportunities for change.

This guide aims to set out good project management practice. It takes you step by step through the necessary planning and implementation of a project in more or less chronological order and helps you to avoid the pitfalls. It suggests what needs to be done at each stage to minimise future problems and to smooth the progress of the work. At the same time it gives advice about ensuring that all concerned are aware of what is happening, and what **should** be happening. These two should be the same, of course, but too often are not. Various techniques will be referred to in the course of this progress: where necessary, a reference will be given to the appropriate guide in this series.

1.2	**What is a project?**	There are a number of project definitions in use, covering a very wide range of activities from a single task to be performed by one person, to a programme running for several years. For the purposes of this guide, an IS project is a process whereby a defined, unique, information system, or a self-contained part of an information system, is produced to a defined quality within a finite timescale and using allocated resources. This means that:

- all concerned will know what is to be produced and can recognise whether it has (or has not) been produced;

- there is a specified date for completion so that the project does not just drift on indefinitely;

- account is taken of resources available.

The subject of an IS project might be a Feasibility Study, a Full Study, a turnkey system, a procurement or a Strategy Study as well as the traditional IS development and implementation.

> While there are many common features to projects, there are also differences between them. These differences make every project unique, and give rise to the risks inherent in every project. It is these differences, and the fact that projects are endeavouring to produce something which did not exist before, which lead to the need to use project management techniques.

1.3	**The aim of project management**	What, then, is the aim of project management? First and foremost, it is to deliver a specified product, of the required quality, to the people who need it, at the agreed time and within the agreed budget. That means the whole product as currently specified. The benefits of successful project management follow from this aim. They are:

- the work is carried out on schedule, without unforeseen and annoying delays;

- there will be no need for expensive redesign of the system or expensive reworking of items already completed (or thought to have been completed);

- the risks to the project are managed and controlled so that the opportunities and benefits are fully realised;

- the quality of the resulting system is such that the users will be able to work with the minimum of interruptions caused by malfunction or failure.

Project management techniques structure a project into smaller, normally consecutive, blocks which are referred to as **stages** in this guide. This follows the management principle that large problems become easier to solve if they are broken down into a number of smaller ones.

Each project will have a person in charge, who may or may not be supported and assisted by managers of the separate stages. The PRINCE documentation (see 1.4) defines a Project Manager and a Stage Manager. To cover both of these situations, the term 'Project Manager' is used in this guide.

1.4	**Consistent with PROMPT and PRINCE**	The PROMPT project management method was adopted as the standard method within government, and has subsequently been enhanced and renamed PRINCE. This guide is consistent with both.` It does not replace either: PRINCE and this guide are complementary. It is inevitable that PROMPT/PRINCE terms will be used in the guide. When this happens, they will be explained. A description of PRINCE is given at Annex A; if you are not familiar with the method, reading the annex will be time well spent.
1.5	**Where are project management methods not appropriate?**	You will see from the definition of a project above that not **everything** is a project. Project management techniques are not appropriate to a continuing task with no foreseeable end. Examples would be managing, after it has been provided, a production type of environment, where work flows in, is processed and passed on, or returned to the originator. This happens with a library or typing or printing service, or when dealing with members of the public calling at the office. These management tasks need other techniques.

If the project is very small, say less than about 12 man months' work, then the principles set out in this guide should be followed, but the practices should be modified to tailor the cost to reflect the cost of the project. Advice on such projects is given in *Guide D1: Small Systems*.

2   The information system lifecycle

2.1   The lifecycle

The lifecycle of an information system (see Fig 2a) will normally start during a Strategy Study, when a need or opportunity is identified. The first ideas will be refined and included in the project portfolio supporting the strategy. Where it is thought that information technology might be used, the ideas will be developed through the Feasibility Study and the Full Study, both of which will be managed as projects. If the results of the studies are favourable, a system development project is initiated. This may or may not include procurement of hardware and/or software. The development may be done in-house, or by an outside body (turnkey development) after which the complete system is handed over to the users and maintenance staff. Thereafter it will be in operation, subject to maintenance and revision, until eventually it is discarded or replaced.

During the 'operation, maintenance and revision' part of the cycle, need for enhancements may arise, which may well generate further development projects. These projects will themselves pass through elements of the same cycle. They will produce sub-systems which are accepted as part of the parent system, or they will produce new systems in their own right. Note that there may be refinements of scope, deliverables and cost constraints, exercised through controls imposed by the IT Executive Committee on the Project Board.

Alternatively, the project may be the procurement of a facilities management arrangement, where an outside body provides a service and operates the system on the department's behalf. See *Guide E4: Facilities Management*. Overviews of the elements in the cycle are set out in Fig 2a.

Fig 2a Lifecycle of an Information System

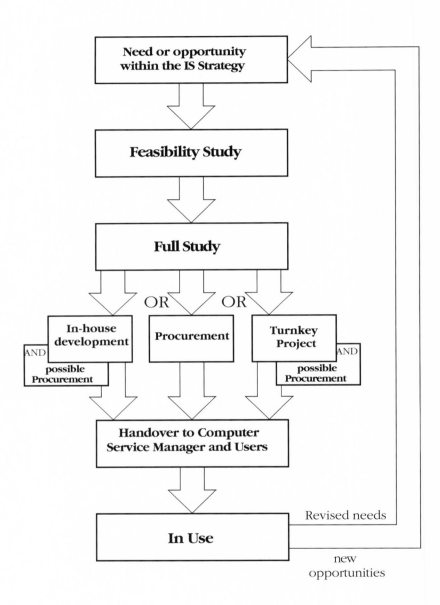

2.1.1   IS Strategy

An IS Strategy provides a statement from top management and a published consensus of the role of IS in the organisation. It includes an identification of the major requirements for resources and investment over the medium term. The strategy also establishes a framework for setting priorities. It sets the ground rules and standards to create the environment for taking decisions on individual projects.

2.1.2   Feasibility Study

Once the potential for an information study system is identified during a strategy study, and accepted, it will be included in the project portfolio. It will be supported at first by broad estimates of the cost, timescale and benefits. Thereafter, the project details will be progressively developed and estimates refined until the required facility is installed and in use or the project abandoned (see Fig 2b). The first step will be a **Feasibility Study**, during which the requirement will be defined, and an examination made of practicable solutions, both IT and non-IT based. This will draw on an examination of any existing system provided. The study should concentrate on the broad outlines of possible systems. It should make such estimates of staff, equipment and other resources as are necessary and possible to enable a recommendation to be made whether the proposal is likely to be technically possible and commercially sensible and whether to go further and undertake a Full Study. The requirements of a subsequent Full Study (see below) should be borne in mind while conducting the Feasibility Study to minimise the risk that work done will need to be redone later. If a Full Study is recommended, an estimate of its cost should be included in the Feasibility Study report. For more information see *Guide B2: The Feasibility Study*.

Fig 2b: Project Management within the Information System Strategy

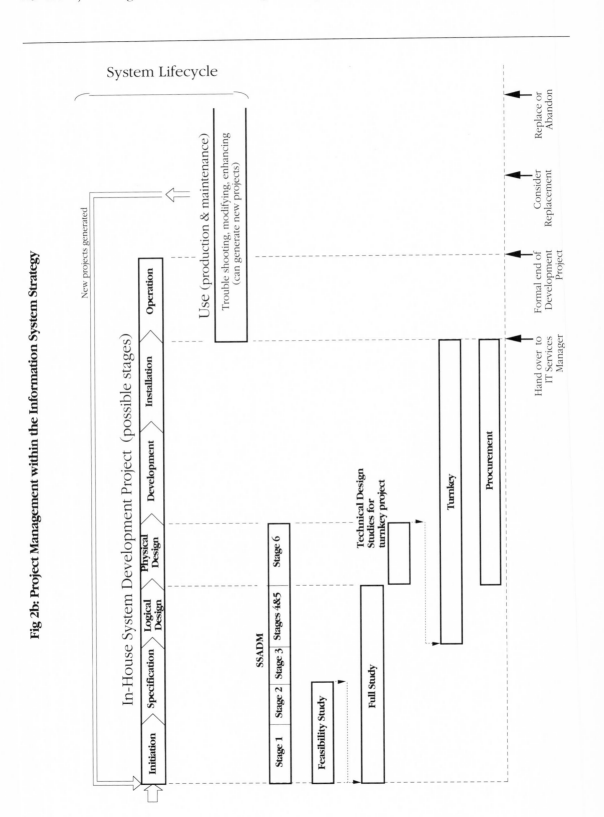

2.1.3   Full Study

If the proposal is feasible, the next task is to establish in detail exactly what is required, and the ways in which it can be achieved. For this it is necessary to authorise expenditure on, and commit resources to undertake, a **Full Study**. During the course of the study, the team needs to establish the detailed business requirements and confirm that the investment in the project is likely to represent good value for money (the investment appraisal). They will produce:

- a project plan for the remainder of the development work showing what stages would be desirable in the project, if approved;

- an Operational Requirement (OR) if any part of the project (hardware, software or personnel) is to be obtained from outside the department;

- a plan for evaluating the response to the OR.

For more information, see *Guide B3: The Full Study.*

The Full Study uses few staff relative to the development work which may follow. However, if the Full Study recommendations are accepted it will lead to commitment of a much greater level of resources on the development work. It is, therefore, not worth undertaking the Full Study unless there are good prospects that staff and money will be available for the prospective project itself. This means ensuring that sufficient numbers of staff with appropriate skills will be available for an in-house development, or that it is possible to contract out the work. In this context the time which will elapse from end of Full Study to availability of resources must be borne in mind.

Experience has shown that the success of IS projects is greatly influenced by the quality of the Full Study. Deficiencies arising from mistakes and omissions in the specification and design work of the Full Study are difficult, and therefore expensive, to correct later. It is thus **essential** to employ good quality, experienced staff for the study, and to ensure that they work within adequate quality control, change control and management control procedures. These are all dealt with in later sections of this guide.

The Full Study team will consider, in the light of the departmental IS Strategy, and recommend one of the following:

- in-house development

- purchase of a suitable package

- development and supply by consultant or software house - turnkey approach.

Each of these courses may or may not include the procurement of hardware.

| 2.2 | **In-house development** | This guide is mainly concerned with managing an in-house IS development project, but the principles apply to any type of IS project. Problems peculiar to specific types of project are mentioned in chapter 10. |

2.2   In-house development

This guide is mainly concerned with managing an in-house IS development project, but the principles apply to any type of IS project. Problems peculiar to specific types of project are mentioned in chapter 10.

2.3   Buying a suitable package

Buying a suitable package has many attractions, but ready-made solutions are seldom exactly what is required. There is often a need to write programs to provide links with the existing departmental system, or to modify departmental requirements to match the facilities provided by the package. The cost and time of making these adaptations must be taken account of in the investment appraisal and planning processes.

2.4   Procurement

It may be necessary to purchase, lease or hire equipment on which to run the information system being developed. If a procurement is required which involves little work then it is easier to control if it is included as part of the development work. A more substantial procurement should be treated as a separate project, using specialist procurement staff. In this case work to construct or adapt a building should then be part of the procurement project. Particular care needs to be taken over liaison and information flows between the procurement project on the one hand, and the project for software development or purchase on the other hand. This is to ensure that the time of delivery of the equipment and of the software are matched, and that the two are compatible when they are put together.

The same considerations apply when replacing existing equipment where the replacement is expected to support the same software system as the old. It is seldom possible for the application software to be transferred without some modification. For more information, see *Guide B6: Procurement*.

| 2.4.1 | Turnkey system or Facilities Management approach | Lack of staff, or lack of staff with the appropriate skills, may necessitate adopting a turnkey solution or a Facilities Management solution. For a turnkey system an outside contractor, software house, consultant or manufacturer, or any combination of these, is required to produce and install a system to meet departmental needs. A Facilities Management solution is where a contractor supplies a **service**, or operates the system on behalf of the department. While these solutions have their attractions, beware of assuming that nothing has to be done within the department. The project must still be managed. You must specify the departmental requirements and ensure that the product delivered meets those requirements; there is preparatory work needed within the department, such as training or redeployment of staff; and there will need to be progress meetings between the department and the supplier. All of these factors decree that someone within the department must be in charge of the departmental activities. A Project Manager must be appointed at the earliest possible moment, and may well be a senior manager from the business area supported by the department's IT specialists. Since there may be more activities to manage than if the work were carried out in-house, there is greater need than usual for competent project management. |

For more information, see *Guide E3: Turnkey Projects*.

| **2.5** | **How many projects?** | The Feasibility Study, Full Study and subsequent system development can, and should, each be managed as discrete projects. Additionally, major programmes should be broken into a number of self-contained projects wherever possible, to ease management problems, rather than leave the programme to be managed as one huge project. Each project then has its own boundaries and identified objectives. The in-house development and the procurement may be managed as one project or as separate projects. There are advantages and disadvantages in both: where the balance of advantage lies depends mainly on the size and complexity of the procurement. |

Further information can be found in Chapter 10. Guidance on the appropriate project stages and end products, and on the various types of development projects, can be found in the PRINCE manuals.

| 2.6 | **The size of a project** | It is difficult to give guidance on the optimum size for a project, but the following are general rules. |

- Small is better than large. A small project is easier to manage, so it may well be possible to allocate its management to less experienced or more junior staff, so releasing the pressure on experienced senior staff and providing training for succession.

- The optimum team size seems to be five or six people, and is the size that team members tend to like. More brings communication problems, and fewer makes for difficulty in providing the necessary diversity of skill types and personality types. There will probably be a number of such teams within a project.

- Short is better than long. There is less chance in a short project that unforeseen events will arise to cause disruption. A duration of not more than 18 months should be aimed for and in no circumstances should a project (as defined in 1.2) ever exceed two years.

- No stage in a project should exceed six months if this can be avoided, since detail planning is difficult so far ahead.

| 2.7 | **Handover to users and service managers** | Once the project is completed, the system needs to be put into operational use. There is therefore a need for final acceptance by the business management and by those who have to use it. There is also a need for assignment of operational support responsibility to those who will maintain it in good order. It is important that putting the system into operational use is a formal process. However it should contain no surprises for those people, since they should have been involved in all, or most, stages of the project's development and will have contributed as necessary to its success. |

The need for maintenance and revision inevitably arises after the handover. These processes are undertaken more easily and more cheaply if adequate records were kept during project development of **what** was done, **how** it was done, and **why** it was done that way. Also maintenance will be needed less frequently if quality was controlled properly during development.

2.8 **Security - the place of CRAMM in the project**

Like quality, security is best **designed into** the system. The CCTA Risk Analysis and Management Methodology (CRAMM) is a three stage approach intended to help identify the countermeasures needed to protect the system. These countermeasures should be included in the specification of the project.

Further details can be found in the CCTA publications *CRAMM, the CCTA Risk Analysis and Management Methodology* and *A guide to CRAMM for Management.*.

Part B   Managing the Project

3   People in the project

The management structure is shown in Fig 3.

3.1   The Project Board   At times during the life of a project, there is a need for a forum for:

- assessing the progress made;

- checking that the project is meeting the business needs of the user;

- making high level or policy decisions;

- reconciling the needs of the various interests in a project;

- ensuring that the project is run as a joint venture by the IT specialists and the user specialists, and that both interests are given full recognition;

- ensuring that the department gets good value for money from the project.

To achieve these ends, the IT Executive Committee (ITEC) appoints senior staff to a Project Board for each project to represent the interests of the User Division(s), the IS Division and of the business of the department as a whole. Normally, each of these interests is represented by separate people. In some circumstances one role may need to be filled by two or three people (eg where one person cannot be identified to represent all of the user interests adequately).

Fig 3   Management Structure

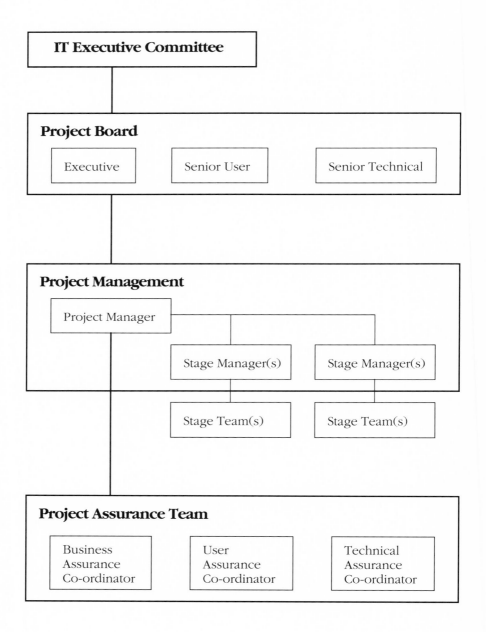

3.2	**The Project Manager**	There are a number of prerequisites for any project to succeed, or even for it to be able to start. One of these is that there should be one person (and only one person) in charge of the day-to-day work. Another is that everybody should know who that person is and, therefore, who to turn to for leadership, for information and for decisions. It is therefore necessary to appoint a manager who will be in day-to-day control of the project, and whose task will be to ensure that the project objectives are met within the constraints set by the Project Board. This manager may be appointed for the duration of the project (a Project Manager) or there may be a succession of people each managing one part, or stage of the project (Stage Managers) who also take on the role of Project Manager. The tasks which should be allocated to these people and the arguments for using one or more people are set out in the PRINCE manuals.
3.2.1	Selecting the Project Manager	It has been said that the best approach to successful project management and control is the employment of an experienced computer professional who is also a good manager. While there is a great deal of truth in this, it must be remembered that some stages of an IS project are not predominantly IT in scope, eg specification of requirements. Other skills, including those related to the business aspects, are therefore needed for those stages, and must be available.
3.2.2	Skills and experience required	A Project Manager needs to have good communication, decision making and interpersonal skills. He/she should have received formal training in project management methods and procedures, including PRINCE, and should ideally have at least two years' experience in management of part of an IS project. He/she should also have received formal training in SSADM and have had experience in its use because he/she will be managing people who are using SSADM.

Project Managers should be people with experience both as team leaders and in the Project Support Office. Every effort should be made during the course of a project to identify the future Project Managers and to encourage their development. In the meantime, they should be employed on smaller, and less critical, projects and be supported by the most experienced teams, and with an experienced Project Board.

3.3	**Project Assurance Team**	One of the prime objectives of the Project Manager is to produce the end products on time, within budget and to the required **quality standard**. To help with this, an independent team should be appointed for the duration of the project to ensure that the departmental quality standards are applied to the project, and that project quality standards are applied to the individual end products. This team is known as the Project Assurance Team (PAT) in PRINCE. Its activities cross stage boundaries and divide into three roles, responsible for the following.

1   **Business aspects**, eg:

- assisting with project planning, monitoring expenditure and progress to ensure that the financial integrity of the project is maintained;
- ensuring that the Investment Appraisal (IA) is amended whenever it is affected by a change to the project, to allow checks to be made that the project will still achieve the desired returns;
- co-ordinating quality reviews and technical exception activities;
- maintaining the administrative structure.

2   **User aspects**, eg ensuring that:

- the users at all appropriate levels are involved in the project,
- all concerned with the project are aware of the business needs and of the human factor issues;
- user acceptance criteria are established; that user needs are met;
- that conversion and recovery procedures are in place;
- that test data is available when needed.

3   **Technical aspects**, such as:

- ensuring the technical integrity of the project;
- advising on quality criteria;
- ensuring conformance with standards;
- applying technical control methods and technical exception procedures.

| 3.3.1 | Project Support Office | If there is more than a very small number of projects, it is best to centralise the various business and technical assurance duties in a Project Support Office. This concentrates the expertise in one location, facilitates the cross-fertilisation of ideas between projects, and makes it easier to provide machine support for the PAT. It also provides a single point for collection of project related information, for the benefit of all projects and for use in development and control of the strategy. |

3.4 Allocation of tasks

Guidance on the duties and tasks to be allocated to the people and groups referred to above and on their responsibilities is given in the PRINCE manuals.

3.5 Project teams

The Project Manager of any project is be supported by teams each of which is likely to have its own team leader. These teams are drawn from the appropriate IT and business areas, and probably from other specialist areas such as organisation and methods or telecommunications.

4   Project team building

4.1   Management of users' and IT staff

The Project Manager's task is made easier if staff from the business area and the IT area are formally allocated to the project by name and for specific periods detailed in the project resource plans. This formal allocation must, of course, be with the agreement of the appropriate line managers and, preferably, of the staff themselves. Negotiating this agreed allocation is part of the task of planning the project.

There are two consequences of such action:

- If the project starts to depart from the agreed time schedule, it may be necessary to renegotiate the allocation.

- Some specialist resources, eg database manager and telecommunication specialists, may be needed for only a short period, at a time which cannot be forecasted very accurately when the project is being planned. In these circumstances, a 'window' should be negotiated when the specialist is prepared to allocate the required amount of time. Thereafter, the Project Manager and the specialist should keep in touch about progress and the exact requirement for the project.

The principle should be observed as nearly as possible for **all** staff who will work on the project, including contractor and consultant staff. (See 4.2 below.)

4.1.1   Partnership between user and technical staff

The project organisation is a partnership between business specialists and technical specialists, and the Project Manager must ensure that neither of these is a sleeping partner. Both partners must accept that they have a part to play, and that this involves committing resources to the project, at the time and on the scale agreed when the plans were prepared.

4.1.2   How should users participate?

The Business Manager and his or her staff need to participate from the very start of project planning. This means taking a full and active part in project teams to ensure that business needs are met and participating in any discussion where compromise is necessary. The Business Manager will also need to provide a member for both the Project Board and the project assurance team.

4.1.3   The Business Manager's responsibilities

The Business Manager's first responsibility is to define his/her requirements adequately and unambiguously. Failure to do this is certain to lead to disappointment with the product eventually delivered. The work of investigating the present system, if any, and defining the requirement in detail will probably be carried out by SSADM or COMPACT specialists from the IT Directorate. However the Business Manager must:

- make staff available for consultation;

- check that information about the present system and future needs has been transmitted correctly, understood, and recorded accurately. This will entail some effort in understanding the SSADM process and conventions;

- provide staff to undertake quality reviews at appropriate times;

- prepare acceptance criteria for the desired system, and test data to check whether the system will meet the acceptance criteria;

- take part in acceptance testing;

- release staff for training to use the new system when it is delivered, and maybe for the changeover (eg of records) to the new method of working.

All of these activities will be a considerable drain on resources, but it is in the Business Manager's interests to ensure that good staff with appropriate knowledge are seconded to the project team.

4.1.4   If the Business Manager cannot participate

Staff from the business area may consider that they cannot participate fully in the work of the project because there is an existing system to be managed and staffed and there are problems in releasing resources. However, it is essential for the success of the project that **Business Managers and potential users** are fully committed to and involved in the project. They should be encouraged to treat their involvement as an investment for the future (see *Guide B1: The User's Role in System Development*). If they cannot do so, you must consider:

- whether the project should be undertaken at all;

- what action can be taken to help the future users continue their day-to-day work while still participating fully in the project.

Action taken might be:

- to agree overtime working with the staff;

- to let a contract to manage the existing facility while the replacement system is being developed.

A third course of action is a possibility, if staff changes are expected in the business area.

- Use incoming staff as business area representatives on the project.

This last course of action has its dangers and must be used with caution. While it does involve the new staff in development of the new system, they may not have the necessary experience in the workings of the organisation, nor the necessary background.

In all three cases, the costs need to be included in the investment appraisal for the project and justified in the same way as any other expenditure.

4.1.5	What happens if the Business Manager does not participate?	The expected users may experience uncertainty, lack of interest and perhaps fear when the system is delivered if they were not actively involved in developing it. This can reduce motivation and morale and perhaps cause physical withdrawal such as absenteeism. The overall effect is that the new system operates at a reduced efficiency and subsequent projects may be met with increased resistance.
4.1.6	Technical responsibilities	The prime responsibility of the technical specialists is to deliver the specified system on time and within budget, **knowing that it will be acceptable.** To do this, they must know what the Business Manager really needs. This requires careful analysis of his/her wants, discussion with the users, and probably a degree of education of the Business Manager and user. This ensures that each partner knows and understands the other's methods, conventions and terminology. While the IT Directorate often needs to take the initiative in technical education, it must also be open to receive comments, advice and constructive criticism from the users.

The IT Directorate needs to ensure that there is a set of standards in place for specifying, designing, developing and implementing the project. These must be known and understood by the whole team. The team should be aware of the importance of standards to the departmental IT strategy. They must also know about the legal requirements which make it mandatory under certain circumstances to refer to standards in public procurement.

An approach similar to that set out in 4.1.4 should be taken when considering competing demands for system development staff and specialists such as database managers or telecommunications staff. In these cases, it may be possible to meet the need by engaging consultants, software contract staff etc.

| 4.1.7 | Project Manager's responsibilities |

Staff are the key to success or failure of any project. It is most important, therefore, that Project Managers are as fully informed as possible about the human aspects of the implementation of IS. They must pay due attention to human factors such as:

- proper training and motivation of both development and user staff;

- the design of jobs;

- providing appropriate environmental conditions (even temperatures, adequate lighting etc); and a well-designed, ergonomic workstation (VDU, keyboard, desk and adjustable chair);

- designing systems with the users' needs uppermost in mind.

Experience has shown that such considerations make a major contribution both to productivity and to the well-being of staff. This is not just a 'management cares' issue, it is essentially a strategic one: morale of people and the efficiency of business go hand-in-hand. The Project Manager must take responsibility for ensuring that human factors are considered at the earliest stage. Human factors (or ergonomics) must be catered for otherwise the full potential of systems is unlikely to be achieved.

The joint report on *Ergonomic Factors Associated with the Use of Visual Display Units* produced in May 1988 by CCTA and the Council of Civil Service Unions (CCSU) is a useful starting point.

4.2	**Managing consultants and other external resources**	At times, the numbers of staff or the skills needed for the project may not be available. Consultants or contract staff may therefore be needed. These resources must be costed, planned for (including any lead time) and managed in much the same way as directly employed staff. This means that an agreed schedule of dates is required when the resources will be made available, and arrangements must be made for quality control of their end-products, reporting arrangements for actual and expected progress, highlight reports, etc. In return, the consultants and contractors will want to know what project management and quality control methods, analysis techniques, etc, will be in use on the project, and the way in which the company is expected to interface with them. Arrangements for all of these should be included in any invitations to tender sent out, and in their contracts. Further information is given in *Guide E1: The Information Systems Services industry*.
4.3	**Team relationships**	Project teams will vary according to the demands of the task and the stage of the project. However a cohesive group is more easy to form if the team membership is not changed.

Difficulties between individuals with different professional backgrounds and skills may arise through ineffective communication, and differences in approach or interest. This may be because the non-technical staff initially have little understanding of the technical aspects of the project. Equally the technical specialists may have little understanding of the users' needs. Reluctance of a user manager to take part in decision-making on issues involving technical aspects of the project may reduce the confidence of the specialist. In turn, this may affect whether the users' contribution is accepted and acted upon. Similarly, the non-specialist may lack confidence in the technical staff if the latter are concerned with simply making the computers more efficient, rather than making them more effective for the users' needs.

Past experience of working in mixed project teams will affect the ease with which team members relate to each other. If users are involved in the planning and design stages of the project, the experience gained will enable technical and non-technical specialists to cope with problems and to resolve the conflicts which often arise. Discouraging the user from participating in IS projects may appear to be easier at the outset but such an approach will do nothing to improve communication or the quality of the system. On the contrary, it will ensure failure.

4.3.1	Matching personalities	It is not always possible to match personality types with particular task roles to form an effective team, given the available human resources and the technical skills demanded by the project, but the attempt should be made. Knowledge of individuals who have worked together on previous projects may help in making staff selections. Personality questionnaires, as used by psychologists and by human resource consultants, can be used in team development to give a rough measure of personality.

On occasions, personality clashes may arise. Difficult team members may either respond to an authoritarian approach from the project leader or may best be controlled by the influence of other team members.

4.3.2	Team building	When all the people required for the project have been selected and allocated, **the Project Manager needs to build them into a team.** This is to ensure smooth working and co-operation, rather than conflict, between the project personnel.

4.3.3	Motivating the team	Motivating the project team is very important at any time, and particularly so when a project has problems or difficulties. Clearly defined targets or deadlines help increase motivation, as does job satisfaction. This can be gained by selecting appropriate people for the task at project initiation. The tasks which people enjoy doing usually, but not necessarily, coincide with what they are good at.

Team members themselves are likely to have a deeper understanding than the Project Manager of the nature of the work and the likely problems. Participation in target setting will therefore help the acceptance of the targets and provide the motivation to work towards them. More realistic work schedules can be evolved when staff have a chance to estimate the length of time required to complete the work. The Project Manager should, however, bear in mind that research has shown that people tend to underestimate the time and effort needed to complete a task. They should attempt to gain some idea of the criteria on which staff are basing their estimates. This will further the understanding of the task, important if and when problems arise which affect the running of the project.

The Project Manager can improve team spirit by being responsive to requests for help and advice from team members; problems should be discussed openly with a view to overcoming the difficulties, rather than to placing any blame. Above all, he should be **visible**.

Teams should be motivated by persuasion and explanation; this reflects a democratic management style and is usually successful in avoiding conflicts and resentment. It may be most effective, for example, during the planning stages of the project when views and ideas are required and for improving quality or productivity. An authoritarian approach on the other hand may be most effective when the detailed plans have been finalised or the team is very large.

4.3.4	Conflicts with other needs	During the process of team building, the needs of the project are often found to clash with other requirements within the department. These might include the need to continue the users' day-to-day work, the desire to complete other projects and the consideration of future projects. Some of the clashes may be minimised because a level of priority has been assigned to the project in the strategy plan. To resolve other clashes it is first necessary to examine the project in the light of departmental business needs and its supporting IS strategy. Do bear in mind, though, the disruption and delay, and the effect on morale, which would result if it were decided to take staff away from a project which had already started and on which they were already working hard to keep to schedule.
4.4	**Communication**	For effective teamwork, good communication is essential so that team members have access to the right information at the appropriate time. Some project staff will be involved in the planning process itself and will thus have a good understanding of the project. Others will need to be made aware of the various plans and how they fit into them. The Project Manager and the team leaders must be aware of the effectiveness of, and the problems caused by, the office grapevine. News will spread very quickly, but is likely to be distorted, or at least to have interpretations added to it, in its transmission. Formal meetings should be used to convey the correct messages between different planning levels. It is worth considering whether these formal meetings should be supplemented by informal presentations and briefings, to allow feedback, or by a project newsletter.

4.5 Commitment and participation	A cohesive group, whose members are committed to the task and to the team, develops when interactions between members are frequent and the team members share the same or similar task goals. Developing staff commitment can increase the success of the project and the willingness to overcome problems and resistance, as well as improving staff retention. Explaining how the work of team members relates to the success of the project and organisation will indicate to staff that they are valued and will help to foster commitment to the team and to the organisation.
4.5.1 Team meetings	The classic approach to managing a large project, as with many other types of management problem, is to break it down into small self-contained tasks, and to allocate those tasks to small teams. With small groups, there are few problems of communication **within** the team, but it is difficult for any team to keep sight of its position, and the position of its current task, within the whole project organisation. This can lead to a feeling of isolation from the project and to lack of communication to other teams and to the Project Manager, or problems such as falling behind schedule. These effects can be overcome by instituting a periodic meeting of teams, if numbers are small, or of team leaders. These meetings will:

- ensure liaison and communication between teams;

- inform the Project Manager of progress, both to date and expected;

- give timely warning of problems beginning to emerge.

To be effective, team meetings should be held at least once each month, on fixed dates. On the other hand, if they are held more than once a week they become ineffective and are very expensive. The ideal lies somewhere between the two, and depends on the size, importance and stage of the project. In particular, it depends on how quickly significant progress can be made and reported. The team meetings should have a proper agenda and formally recorded decisions about future actions, responsibilities, etc.

The Project Manager should attend the meetings if possible. If there are numerous teams meeting frequently, a member of the Project Assurance Team (see chapter 3) should attend and report to the Project Manager to enable him to formulate his highlight report to the Project Board.

4.5.2	At the team meetings	At the meeting, problems should be reported frankly and objectively to the Project Manager if present, or to the PAT member. The Project Manager must be aware that communications may be distorted especially if the information he is given is incomplete or there seems to be a reluctance to report on progress. Open communication is facilitated if team members do not feel threatened by the likely consequences of reporting or do not fear that the 'bad news' fall on deaf ears. The very nature and complexity of some projects mean that difficulties arise which are not due to the lack of skill or competence of project staff. In truth, problems may be arising from a department's ambitious proposals or from inaccurate project planning. Therefore, a good Project Manager should strive to be approachable, at times sympathetic, assertive and resourceful, depending on the circumstances. Remember that imagined problems are as real as real problems.
		If a team member is expressing emotion (anger, fear) at a meeting, the team leader should be prepared to deal with the feelings rather than keep discussion rigidly to the subject matter and decision-making activities. This will reduce the chance of resentment developing and help smooth the progression to other agenda items.
4.5.3	Who should participate?	Participation in team meetings by all staff concerned with, or affected by, the project will ensure that minority views are expressed and disagreements or problems can be focused upon and solved. Participation in decision-making can induce commitment to the goals of the organisation. People respond better to decisions they have had a role in making than ones which are imposed upon them.
		In the past, the responsibility for planning, design and choice of systems was given to technical groups and specialists. The user generally took no part in those project activities.
		The term 'user' includes those people who request or can authorise the project, managers who will use the output of the system and those individuals who are an integral part of the system eg VDU operators. These groups have differing interests, some of which may conflict. However the participation of the managers of user areas is crucial to the overall project success. Any tendencies to shy away from participating, eg leaving decisions to technical staff because they are perceived as being 'experts', must be discouraged.

31

In mixed teams comprising a range of different skills, and perhaps both civil servants and external consultants, it is often not easy to ensure effective team participation. Team size will also affect the interaction of team members. As the team size increases, it becomes less easy for members to participate, some individuals will interact more than others, some will not participate at all despite having a high level of commitment to the project. **Individuals tend to prefer, and often function better in, small groups** (say five or six) as audience anxiety is less and they can talk and have greater influence over other team members.

Gaining commitment and participation from project staff who join the team for short periods is not easy, especially when individuals are moved from projects in which they are already highly involved. Building co-operative teams rather than competitive teams is therefore desirable; an individual is likely to be induced to work on a project if he or she has the knowledge that a similar favour may be returned at a later stage. However, what motivates one team member may not motivate another; there is no universal solution which can be applied. Generally speaking persuasion, and perhaps negotiation, is preferable to exerting pressure.

4.5.4 Feedback and performance

Feedback and performance are closely related. Performance can be heightened by feedback from team members, especially when the task is complex. When team members can express satisfaction or dissatisfaction about a solution or decision then it is more likely that actions (plans, decisions) will be accepted.

Praise should be given freely when tasks have been completed to a satisfactory level. Positive feedback on performance can be used as a powerful reinforcer and can be an incentive during future work activities. Negative feedback, eg feedback on unsatisfactory progress, if made constructively, can help improve performance. **The absence of feedback can be construed to mean that performance is acceptable, or conversely that the effort is little valued.**

4.6   Training needs

Training should be seen as an integral part of the process of maximising the benefits of the investment in IS. A properly organised training programme, which brings users up to the desired levels of competence and confidence, is essential. The success of a system cannot be achieved without adequate training for all those involved, whether they be analysts, programmers or end-users.

It is assumed here that anyone allocated to the project team has been trained, and has gained at least some experience, in the skills needed for general project work. Thus, analysts will have been trained in SSADM, programmers in the appropriate languages, and users in the skills needed for their normal day-to-day work in the user division. Until they become proficient in their particular skills, they will normally be paired with experienced team members under experienced team leaders. This should all be part of the normal environment in which the people work and projects are managed.

There will frequently be a need for additional training over and above the necessary basic skills. The team members from the user division(s) may have little or no knowledge of IT matters; there may be new and unfamiliar equipment needed for the project; a new and unknown software package may be purchased which needs to be tailored to the users' needs or which needs to have application programs built around it.

The needs for training of team members should be investigated as early as possible in the life of the project possibly before the project starts. It must also be agreed with the appropriate Line Managers. There is then the possibility of fitting the training in at the most convenient time, and before the lack of training or the absence of staff because they are away being trained starts to delay the project. This is particularly important when the skills which need to be learnt are taught at formal courses (eg at the Civil Service College or other training organisation) which may not be held very frequently. Teaching related to specific products is more likely to be available when it is needed, ie when the product is delivered.

If there are a number of people to train, it may be possible to arrange for the training to be carried out on the department's own premises at a lower cost. Where possible, training - particularly the initial stages - should be conducted away from the normal workplace to minimise disruptions.

4.7 Planning for succession

The need to keep a project staffed means planning for succession when it becomes known that staff changes are likely: they most certainly **will** happen. Estimates of time and cost will need revision if an experienced, competent team member is replaced by someone less experienced. It is also necessary to forecast the skills which will be needed later in the project, to ensure that they will be available.

The inevitable disruption caused by staff changes is minimised if adequate time for a proper handover can be allowed. The newcomer is less likely to stay if the transition is difficult, with minimal handover, and he/she is left with poor documentation. A second departure will make the effect of the change even worse.

4.8 Organisational characteristics

Evidence is emerging that the organisational culture (its attitude to IT) can affect the degree of success in introducing new technology and influence the success of projects. For example, organisations in which top-level management become highly involved in the decisions on the use of computers and IS are more likely to implement information systems successfully. This involvement of senior staff is more likely to lead to an organisation which:

- rewards staff for their efforts,

- listens to and encourages new ideas,

- allows personal development,

- gives adequate formal staff training as well as on-the-job training,

- encourages staff participation,

- protects job security,

- has management which plans activities and sets goals which are realistic.

All of the above are factors leading to better motivation of teams. Conversely an organisation is likely to have uncommitted, uninterested project teams if it:

- stifles innovation,

- is resistant to change,

- does not reward staff intrinsically (job satisfaction),

- has poor management skills and sets unrealistic targets,

- makes inefficient use of available and potential human resources,

- gives inadequate training,

4.9   Machine support

Finally, it is necessary to ensure that there is adequate machine support for the project team. Its use must be properly scheduled, so that development work can proceed as planned, with the minimum interference with other projects and no chance of corrupting other data.
When the development work is being done in-house, there are competing demands for support machinery. This is likely to occur whether there is a separate development machine, or space is allocated on the production machine.

Here it is necessary to consult the person responsible for capacity management, to acquaint him/her with the need which is foreseen, and to find out whether the need can be met and what difficulty there is in scheduling machine use at times needed by the project. Scheduling staff resources and machine use must, of course, go hand-in-hand, and it may be necessary to procure a new machine before development can proceed.

5   Starting a project

5.1   The project environment

No project can be developed in a vacuum. If it is to have any chance of starting in the first place, and any chance of being completed successfully, it must be:

- consistent with and support the departmental IS Strategy;

- developed in accordance with departmental standards for such projects;

- capable of running in the environment provided for its operation.

Also the resulting information system must be of an acceptable quality. All of this necessitates a lot of discussion with all of the interested parties. Each of the points raised here is dealt with separately below.

5.1.1   The IS Strategy

The IS Strategy in a department is formulated to support its business strategy (see *Guidelines for Directing Information Systems Strategy* published by CCTA and *Guide A2: Strategic Planning for Information Systems*). No project should be considered unless it can be demonstrated that it supports and is in accordance with the strategy. This does not mean that the strategy is unchangeable: merely that the project must be in accordance with the strategy being applied at the time. But it does mean that projects will have their origins in the formulation of the IS Strategy, or in its periodic updating, and will be included in the resulting project portfolio. If any projects are proposed which do not originate in this way, it is necessary to consult the IS Planning Secretariat (ISPS) before any work is undertaken. This will be done before the Project Manager is appointed, of course, but should be borne in mind whenever changes to the project are being considered.

| 5.1.2 | Standards | For consistency and to enable comparisons to be made, there should be a set of departmentally accepted standards. These specify such things as the format of documentation and what standard of quality will be used to judge the products. If there is no standard adopted within the IT Directorate for development of a particular aspect of an information system, or that standard is out of date, then much time and effort will be expended by each producer of an end-product in designing the products from scratch. It will be very difficult to ensure that the products are consistent and comparable. |

The departmental IS Strategy will indicate which technical standards need to be considered when specifying and procuring systems. Further information about the need for and use of such standards may be found in *Standards Publication (SP) no 4: A Guide to the Requirements of Decision 87/95/EEC*, and in CCTA's *Catalogue of Standards for Use in IT Procurement*. These and other standards guidance material may be obtained from the departmental Standards Liaison Officer or from CCTA.

Once standards have been established, they must be kept up-to-date. This requires feedback from the quality review procedures to the departmental standards officer (or to the Standards Liaison Officer) about any deficiencies or problems found in the standards.

This problem is not peculiar to an IS project, of course, and the IS standards will probably be part of a wider set of standards covering the whole department.

| 5.1.3 | IT Services staff | The IT Services staff will probably be affected during the development of a project, if only because the development work involves use of computer or office systems hardware. They will most certainly be affected after the project is complete, because they then have to manage and maintain the new system. They will need to find capacity to run the new system and may even have to find room for new equipment. For these reasons they should be consulted at a very early date. This will ensure that the new work is compatible with any existing or proposed systems which will run in the same environment, and that maintenance is made as easy as possible. |

5.2   **Constraints on the project**

Few organisations have sufficient resources of every kind needed to undertake all the projects they desire. There are always constraints, and they must be identified, and their effect on the project must be evaluated. In particular, their effect on any deadlines must be identified.

5.2.1   Scarce resources

The most serious constraint is likely to be staff. First, the estimate of the staff resources required must be as accurate as possible. It is then necessary to keep the project staffed at the level estimated, in terms of numbers, skills, training and experience, if there is to be any hope of completing on time and to budget. However, the staff will often be taken from a common pool (eg of analysts, programmers, database specialists) available to all projects, as well as from business areas. There will thus be competition for the scarce resources, and time will need to be spent scheduling the work within a project to the best advantage of all projects. Then the draft plans are revisited when the full effects of each proposal have been analysed, and they are modified to optimise these effects, until the best solution is achieved.

A problem of shortage of resources arises when a project departs from its scheduled dates, and project personnel are not released to fulfil the requirement to work on other projects. Or maybe because they **must** be released before the work is complete. It is imperative that there is a method to recognise probable delays to a project at a very early point and to make these known to the Project Board and to the manager of any other project(s) likely to be affected. (See also Chapter 6: Controlling the Project).

5.2.2   Insufficient resources

If the project plan shows that adequate resources are not available to a project (even if already started) within the planned timescale, there are a number of options to consider.

- Can activities within the project be rearranged to make resources available?

- Can the timescale be extended so that the project can be completed with the available resources?

- Can the start, or the start of the next stage, be deferred? If so, what effect will this have on the completion date of the project, on the business case, bearing in mind the rescheduling of resources necessary, and on the departmental strategy?

- Should resources be taken from another project of lower priority? And will this compromise the tactical plan? If resources are transferred, the project giving them up will need to be rescheduled and the project costs recalculated; the business case will need to be re-examined; and, probably, an exception plan will need to be prepared for that project and approved.

- Should resources be bought in from elsewhere? This may be done by way of a turnkey project, by engaging contract staff or by employing consultants.

- Can the department afford to do all the work proposed? Or can it afford **not** to do the work?

The effect of the preferred option on the project plans (the timing, the cost and the scope) and on other projects must be assessed and appropriate recommendations made to the Project Board.

5.2.3 Deadlines	While considering a proposed project, you will be able to identify certain key dates, or deadlines, which cannot be missed if the project is to succeed. These deadlines may relate to financial year-ends, commencement of new legislation, major staff changes, reorganisation proposals etc. They have the property that to fail to achieve the deadline will result in considerable extra delays (eg waiting for the start of the following financial year), extra expense and much embarrassment. You should therefore seek out and record all such deadline dates, then build them into the plans and schedule resources to take account of them. Thereafter, a major objective of the communication and control process is to keep the deadlines at the forefront of people's minds, and to control the project to ensure that deadlines are met.
	The existence of such deadlines, and the need to control the projects to meet them, will have a management cost in time and money. The existence of this cost must be recognised and taken into account in the project plans.
5.2.4 Other constraints	Other constraints are likely to be as follows.
	Accommodation: to house the project staff, or the hardware, or the operations and user staff.
	Hardware: whether for project development or for subsequent operation of the system.

Logical dependencies: which will require activities to be performed in certain orders. These orders must be recognised, and built into the project network as it is developed.

The Organisation: which also has a call on the resources which you wish to use, and will prevent a complete freedom of choice when scheduling starts.

Staff: are there sufficient numbers, or appropriate types of skill and experience, or a high enough level of skill? If not, what can be done about it?

Standards: as described at 5.1.2 may appear to reduce freedom of choice. However, use of standards can ensure consistency, quality and comparability of output. It can also remove the need to develop special standards for the project. Use of technical standards should extend freedom of choice in the procurement process.

Time: which needs to be set against the staff numbers, when assessing whether deadlines can be met. But beware of assuming a direct relationship between time and staff resources. Doubling the number of people does not normally halve the time, even if the right mix of skills is available.

Once the constraints are identified and evaluated, they and their effects should be recorded in the Project Initiation Document (see 5.3.4).

| 5.3 | **Defining the project** | When people consider whether a project should be undertaken, there will be a number of opinions, and probably much discussion, about what should be included and what facilities or processes should be provided. While this must be so, it is essential to define the scope of the project carefully before approval is finally sought to spend time or money on it. |

| 5.3.1 | Project boundaries | In defining the scope, consider the project's boundary with surrounding systems (both IT systems and others), and its place within the department's development programme. There should be no overlap with such systems, and no unintentional gaps should be left. As part of such definition, you must consider whether to record what is **not** within the scope of the project, and whether this will avoid misunderstandings resulting from recollections of the early discussion. |

| 5.3.2 | Common definition of objectives | During this process of defining the project boundaries the people involved will start to define their own (personal or branch) objectives relating to the project. These may be hidden or made known; they can be quite diverse and may well be contradictory. It is necessary at a very early point in the project preparation to identify what the **project** objectives are, and then to seek agreement **and acceptance** of these objectives by all project staff and, just as important, by people outside the project who will be affected by it. In defining the objectives, it is best to define them in terms of the end-product(s) needed to support the business need. Once agreed, they are incorporated in the Project Initiation Document for approval by the Project Board. |

5.3.3   Product breakdown structures

Many types of product are common to all, or at least to many, IS projects. For example, it is always necessary to have a definition of the user's business requirements; and there must be agreement on how the project is to be managed and controlled. Other items (invitations to tender, or the specification for a new database) occur frequently but not in all projects; while yet other items occur only rarely.

Any of these items can be defined afresh for each new project. However, effort can be saved if the commonly occurring items are defined as standard product breakdown structures.

- The top level is a general description of a major end-product (Operational Requirement, system test strategy, etc).

- The major products should then be sub-divided as necessary.

- The bottom level is a list of component products such that the amount of work needed to produce each of them, (from the previous component) represents one to two weeks' work for one person or for a small team.

Standard hierarchies can be stored and selected as needed for new projects, as in many project support tools. This process reduces the chance of missing a vital step in planning a project. It reduces the amount of work necessary during the planning, since it is only the unusual products which need to be defined and broken-down afresh. Even these need only be done the first time they occur: thereafter, they can be stored until needed again. Together with configuration management, the product breakdown structure makes it easier to adjust the size of a project at a later stage, or to evaluate a request for a change. This is because it is implicit that cross references will be provided by one or the other (or more likely both) to all related end-products.

When the structure has been defined, the activities needed to deliver the end-product can be assessed, in terms of skill type, quantity and quality. The necessary configuration management can then be introduced (see section 7.6). It will not be possible to define the activities in terms suitable for use on all projects, since projects vary in size, and the quality specification needs to be matched to the proposed use, eg a level of precision which would be needed in a payroll system would not be necessary in long-term weather forecasts.

5.3.4 Project Initiation Document

The decisions about the scope of the project, and approval to move to the next part of the cycle, should lead to a Project Initiation Document. This will contain:

- the project definition, as recorded in the strategy plan and the supporting tactical plan, amplified as above;

- the aims and objectives of the project;

- the risks, constraints and assumptions;

- the project organisation;

- the quality requirements;

- the Configuration Management arrangements;

- plans showing the timescale, resources needed and the controls.

This Project Initiation Document will form the 'contract' between the Project Board and the Project Manager when it has been approved by the Project Board.

5.4 The planning process

It is worth repeating here that one of the keys to successful project management is to prepare good plans based on good estimates. One of the commonest causes of project failure is bad planning. However, **an out-of-date plan is worse than no plan**, since not only is there no agreement on what should be happening, and no means of control, but people can easily fall into the trap of believing that the plan **is** in fact up-to-date, and waste time trying to follow it.

5.4.1	Priority of the project	It is rare that a project can be run in isolation. Usually there are a number of projects competing for the same scarce resources. Allocation of these resources is made easier by the action of the ISPS in putting all projects, whether already started or proposed, into an agreed order of priority. It is not suggested that this order should be fixed for all time - circumstances will change and it is right that the priorities change with them. But the existence of the order makes other decisions easier; it helps in negotiations between Project Managers or Project Boards, and allows the negotiations at least to start at a suitable level, even if they have to move to a higher level (or to an infrequent meeting of a high-level committee) at a later date.

The degree of priority accorded to the project should be recorded in the Project Initiation Document.

A plan must make the most effective use of resources, and planning a project **must** be the responsibility of the Project Manager. However, the planning process is an iterative one, and may well be delegated to a planning specialist who has the time and the ability to go into considerable detail. It is iterative because inevitably ideas will be changed by the planning process as desirable sequences of activities are compared with staff availability and the requirements of other projects. But gradually plans will be refined and then agreed by all interested parties.

Remember: if a plan is not in writing, it does not exist.

5.4.2	The level of plans	Plans will be prepared at two levels.

- **Project plans** will show the whole project in broad outline to satisfy the needs of the Project Board. They are based on the higher levels of the work breakdown structure model in use.

- **Stage plans** will show in more detail the next stage to be started, for use by the Project Manager. They are based on lower levels of the work breakdown structure.

Each of these levels of plan are subdivided into:

- technical (activity) plans which show what is to be done and when, the standard of product required, and how that standard is achieved;

- resource plans which show who will do it, and the cost.

It is important that the appropriate stage plan includes activities for definition of the size, performance requirements, timescales and time limits, and for quality reviews of products. If it helps communication, detailed plans may also be prepared to show tasks to be undertaken in the next two weeks or so by individuals or small teams.

5.4.3   Developing plans   Once the product breakdown structure and the associated Product Flow Diagram (see Fig 5a) are completed, the first stage of the planning is done, and the boundaries of the project are established. It is then possible to rearrange the information into forms more suitable for management and control of the project, such as:

- project networks

- Gantt charts

- resource plans

- end-product lists

- responsibility lists.

Fig 5a: Product flow diagram for the production of a technical manual

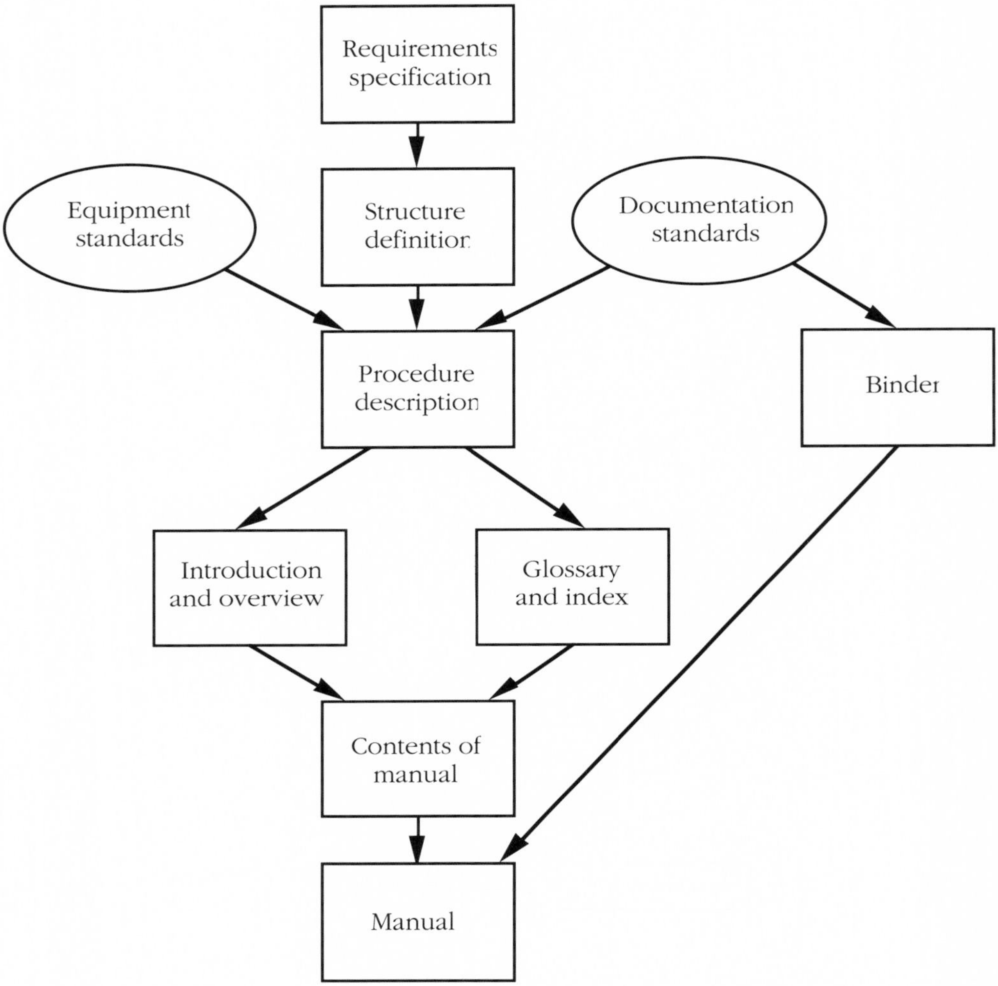

5.4.4   Project networks

The next step is to put the tasks into a logical order and to identify those tasks which can be undertaken simultaneously and those which cannot start until another has finished. This information is best presented as a project network (frequently called a PERT chart) which shows the logical dependencies of all tasks, and which can be expanded to show which is the critical path (or paths). Conversely, the network also shows those activities with 'float', ie those which can be delayed (or where the start of the activity can be deferred) for a period without jeopardising the agreed completion date. But although the critical path is obviously the one on which the Project Manager will concentrate his/her attention, **beware of being complacent about those activities with little float.** This is particularly important where the estimate for the activity is not very reliable for any reason. The mere existence of float will lull people into a false sense of security. Experience has shown that it is these activities which are most likely to delay completion of the project.

Fig 5b: Part of a Small Project Network

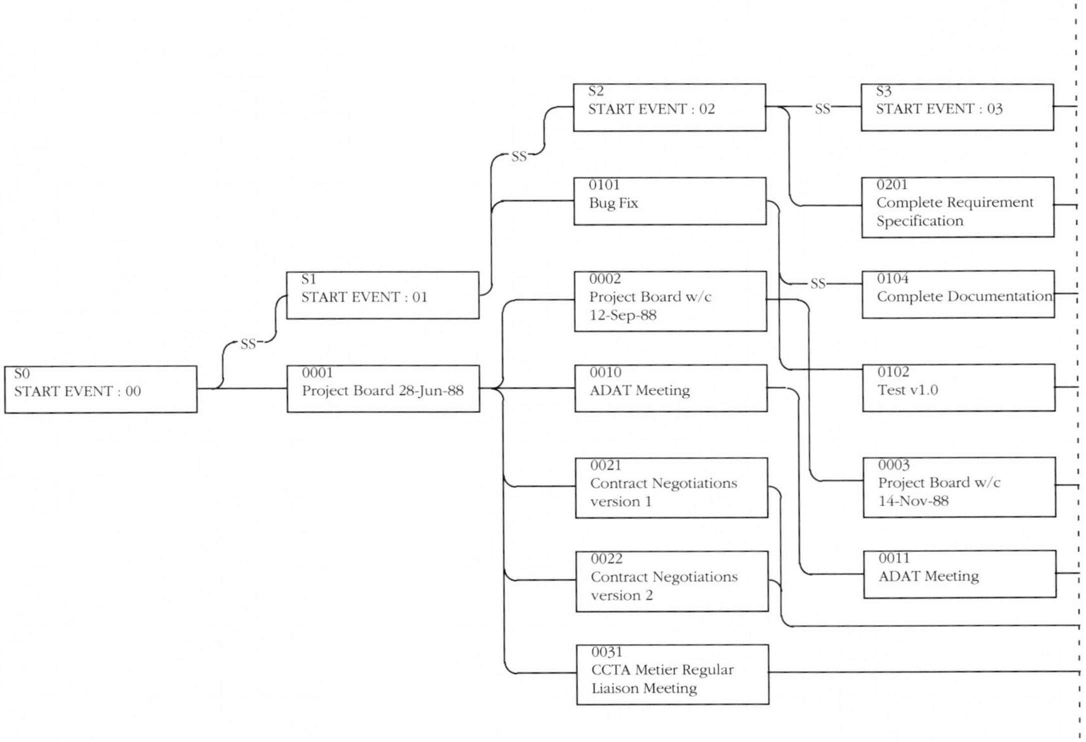

The network is a **planning** tool and no attempt should be made to use it to **control** the project, since it is very difficult in a network to indicate progress other than on completion of an activity. The way to control is to convert the network into a Gantt chart.

| 5.4.5 | Gantt Chart |

The Gantt chart is the technical plan, in PRINCE terms, and is the document to use to show progress. It shows only the timescale, with no resource allocation or usage, so it should be supplemented by a resource plan.

Figure 5c shows an example of a Gantt chart.

Further information on project networks, Gantt charts, resource plans, end-product lists and responsibility lists can be found in Annex C.

**5.5   Quality
         Management**

Quality, like security, is all pervasive and needs to be built into a product, rather than being added as an afterthought. This means that quality must be considered right from the start of a project, and must be considered within the quality assurance environment established as part of the IS Strategy. It must be applied:

• consistently, so that it is capable of repetition;

• to every activity and end-product in the project, so that nothing is left out.

In this connection, an exhaustive checklist is desirable, to avoid disagreements at a later stage, eg when the user complains that the system is slow, although speed was not a part of the agreed specification.

5.5.1   Quality within the
        project

At the start of the project, it is necessary to consider the following.

• How the international, national and departmental standards are to be applied to the project.

• What **level** of quality is needed and is to be included in the specification for the end-products. Too low a level (whether the result of a faulty specification, or of inadequate control) and the products will not be fit for their purpose: too high a level and money and effort are being wasted.

Fig 5c: A Gantt Chart

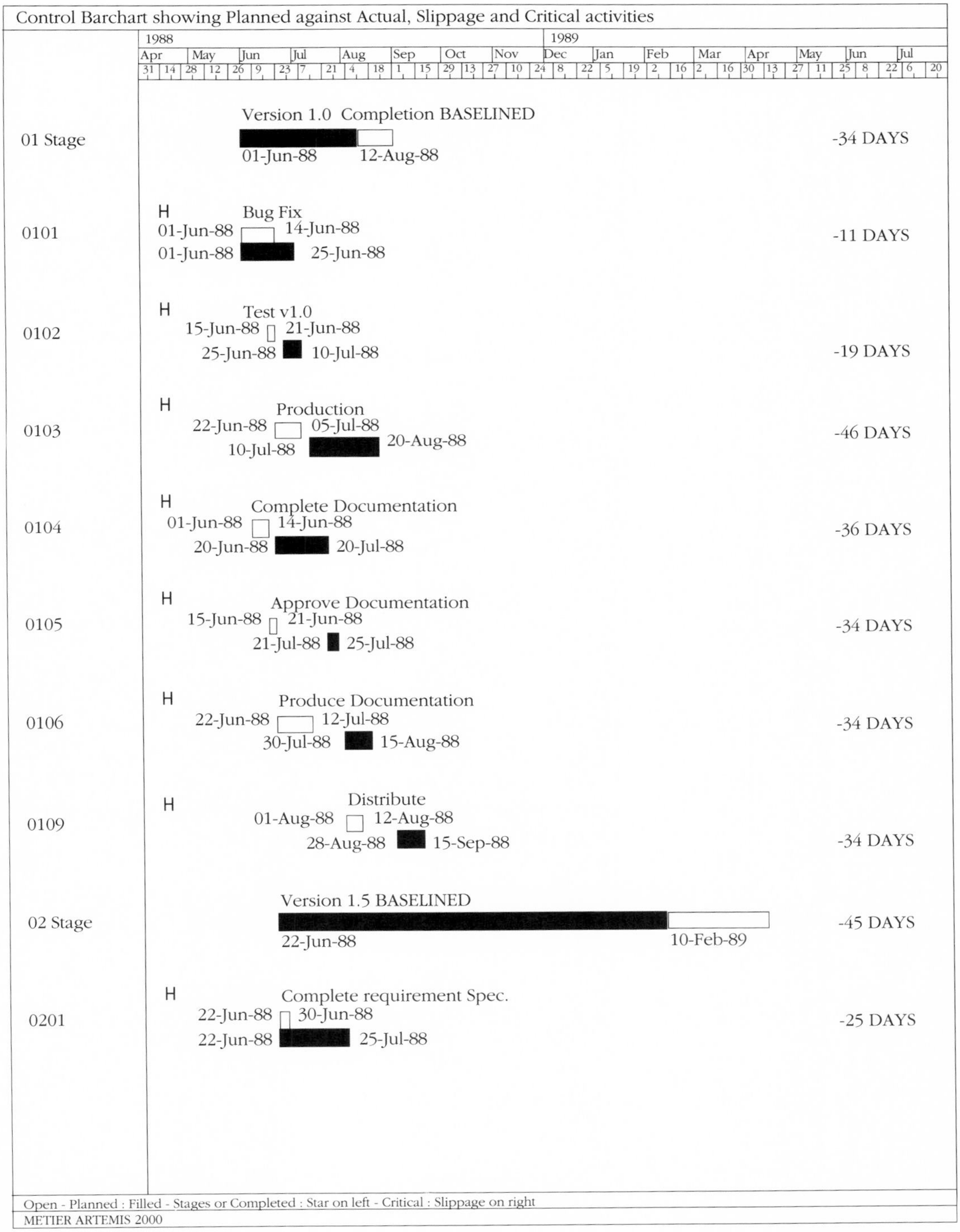

Control Barchart showing Planned against Actual, Slippage and Critical activities

	1988									1989							
	Apr	May	Jun	Jul	Aug	Sep	Oct	Nov	Dec	Jan	Feb	Mar	Apr	May	Jun	Jul	
	31 14	28 12	26 9	23 7	21 4	18 1	15 29	13 27	10 24	8 22	5 19	2 16	2 16	30 13	27 11	25 8	22 6 20

01 Stage — Version 1.0 Completion BASELINED
01-Jun-88 12-Aug-88   -34 DAYS

0101 — H Bug Fix
01-Jun-88 14-Jun-88
01-Jun-88 25-Jun-88   -11 DAYS

0102 — H Test v1.0
15-Jun-88 21-Jun-88
25-Jun-88 10-Jul-88   -19 DAYS

0103 — H Production
22-Jun-88 05-Jul-88
10-Jul-88 20-Aug-88   -46 DAYS

0104 — H Complete Documentation
01-Jun-88 14-Jun-88
20-Jun-88 20-Jul-88   -36 DAYS

0105 — H Approve Documentation
15-Jun-88 21-Jun-88
21-Jul-88 25-Jul-88   -34 DAYS

0106 — H Produce Documentation
22-Jun-88 12-Jul-88
30-Jul-88 15-Aug-88   -34 DAYS

0109 — H Distribute
01-Aug-88 12-Aug-88
28-Aug-88 15-Sep-88   -34 DAYS

02 Stage — Version 1.5 BASELINED
22-Jun-88 10-Feb-89   -45 DAYS

0201 — H Complete requirement Spec.
22-Jun-88 30-Jun-88
22-Jun-88 25-Jul-88   -25 DAYS

Open - Planned : Filled - Stages or Completed : Star on left - Critical : Slippage on right
METIER ARTEMIS 2000

- How the quality can be specified so that it is possible to measure whether the required quality has been delivered.

- How the quality is to be **controlled** to ensure that the required level is delivered, eg by walkthrough, assessment, audit.

The decisions about quality need to be incorporated into the Project Initiation Document along with the associated configuration management arrangements.

When pressure begins to mount to save time and get a project completed quickly, the first casualty is often the standard of the end-products - the quality. However, reducing the effort put into quality control is only putting off the problems to a later date. Faults not found during development are likely to manifest themselves at the most awkward moment, when the developed product has been put into use. They will inevitably take longer and cost more to correct. This tendency to reduce quality standards should be resisted for the very reasons of cost and best use of time, and only accepted after full examination and documentation of the arguments for and against changing them.

5.6   What consultation is necessary?

A large part of a Project Manager's job lies in talking to people - better known as consultation. A key factor in the success of a project is to ensure that all who have a legitimate interest in it, or who are affected by it, are:

- aware of the proposal,

- in agreement with its objectives,

- able and willing to contribute both to the decision making and to the execution of the project.

The first priority is to **contact the user.** This is to ascertain who will be performing key roles such as specifying user requirements, taking major decisions, providing test data, checking the results, and accepting the system. Thereafter, and before detailed work begins, arrangements should be made to identify all who are likely to have an interest in the project, at all levels, and to ensure that consultation takes place with all relevant people. These will include some or all of the following.

IT Services management and maintenance staff: to make sure that they are able to run and maintain the system when it is eventually installed.

data managers: whether users or database controllers, to ensure that the data-related processes in the system being developed are compatible with existing data and with known developments.

data protection specialists: to ensure that nothing is stored in contravention of the Data Protection Act.

Finance or Audit Branch: to ensure that funds are available, and that financial and audit requirements are met.

forms designers: to ensure that any new forms, or changes to existing forms, are considered in good time for delivery when needed, without the need for (expensive) rush printing.

Health and Safety Officer: to ensure that the installation is both safe and seen to be safe.

IS Planning Secretariat: who will give guidance on interpreting the strategy and tactical plans, and on any information needed about the project to help them monitor the tactical plan.

office services staff (accommodation, telephones and office supplies): because most projects affect accommodation in some way, if only because extra power points are needed or existing points need to be moved to the right place.

O & M Branch: who will be interested at two levels. Firstly during the feasibility study when considering whether a non-IT solution is best, and secondly when developing non-IT parts of the agreed project.

Personnel Branch: to tell them what staff will be needed for the project and to warn them about changes to staff numbers and grades which will result from implementation of the system.

previous Project Managers: both personally and through the project evaluation review and post implementation review reports, to check whether anything similar has been done before, and whether there are lessons for the current project.

Project Support Office: who will probably supply some of the project assurance team, help with preparation of plans and undertake other support work.

security staff: to ensure that adequate security measures are built into the proposed system during its development.

Standards Liaison Officer: to ensure that the project follows the departmental IS standards strategy and to obtain advice on IS standards generally, including legal obligations relating to their use in procurement and in technical regulations.

strategic planners: to ensure that the project is in accordance with the departmental IS Strategy (see sub-section 5.1.1).

telecommunications staff: if any new equipment is to be provided, or if additional use is to be made of existing equipment.

Trades Union Side: to ensure that their members' interests are fully considered.

5.6.1   Sources of advice

The Central Computer and Telecommunications Agency (CCTA) exists to provide the help and services that can best be supplied by a central organisation within government. Its business is to supply knowledge and advice about planning, implementation and use of information systems to help departments run their businesses effectively. Project Managers wishing to avail themselves of any of these services should approach CCTA.

Previous Project Managers will have knowledge and experience of general matters, and may well be able to draw attention to similar projects which have been undertaken in the past. At the very least, they will have knowledge of sources of information available, and will be able to warn against some common mistakes.

Project Support Offices will have similar knowledge to previous Project Managers as well as documentation from previous, and current, projects.

Previous Project Evaluation Reports (PERs) and Post Implementation Reviews (PIRs): no project is identical with any other, but few projects are completely different from all others. Similarities with past projects can often be found.

In fact figures from past projects are often incorporated in the estimating portions of project management support tools - see Annex B. Once parts of the project have been identified, whether by discussion with previous Project Managers or by searching databases, which are similar to parts of past projects, the PERs for those past projects should be obtained. These will provide a wealth of information about whether the timetables and resource allocations for the projects were realistic, and whether the management and control procedures were effective. The PIRs will provide information about the specifications and the quality control. Further information about PERs and PIRs is given in Chapter 8.

Suppliers are an obvious source of information about the capabilities of any of their products which might meet the needs of the project, whether those needs are for hardware, software or for consumables. Use should be made of such sources, but there are European Community (EC) and GATT (General Agreement on Tariffs and Trade) procurement rules designed to ensure that no supplier has an unfair advantage over any other when it comes to the time for procurement. You must ensure that discussions with any supplier cannot be construed as giving that supplier inside information, or advance information, which will allow such unfair advantage.

| 5.7 | Costing the project |

From the outset (when considering during the strategy study whether a project should be undertaken), and right through a project, it is necessary to make estimates of the resources needed for the work planned. Management time must be allowed for this. These estimates are successively refined and amplified during the progress through Feasibility Study, Full Study and subsequent stages of the project. It is essential that each successive round of planning and estimating is as accurate as possible. These should bear in mind holiday periods, other foreseeable absences and staff changes. A middle course should be steered between the desires of the Project Manager to have a generous allocation of staff, and of the senior management to spread scarce resources over as many projects as possible. Either course could result in decisions being taken on unsound evidence: on the one hand approval could be refused because the project seemed too expensive: on the other hand, approval could be given on the basis of:

- an unrealistically low estimate for work which eventually turned out to be much more expensive, or:

- an optimistic, and unrealistic, completion date.

Note that research has found that most people **underestimate** the amount of time or resources needed to complete a given task within a project.

5.7.1   Estimating

While making as much use as possible of data from similar past projects, the task of estimating should be tackled in two ways. Firstly, starting from the top, an overall estimate should be made. You may use one of the various project management support tools on the market (see Annex B), many of which contain a database of information about general project types. This data should be modified in the light of experience within the department and of data taken from projects as they are completed.

Secondly, the tasks should be allocated to staff, bearing in mind the skills, level of training and the experience of the individual, the tools available and the relationship between competing demands. The work represents the effort needed to produce each item in the product breakdown structure. The objective is to make each task the responsibility of a single individual (who may, or may not, be supported by a team) and to gain acceptance of, and commitment to, the estimates. The allocation, and the time allowed for each task, should be discussed with the individual responsible for it, and with those undertaking the work, to ensure that the estimates are reasonable and acceptable. They are then aggregated to obtain a total which can be compared with the overall estimate already obtained. The reasons for any discrepancy should be investigated, and any necessary adjustments made.

5.8   Approvals procedures

There is always competition for project resources. You should therefore take care not to reduce the pool of resources by carrying out work without approval. The approval must be given only after consideration of the cost of the work proposed and of the implications of resource usage, effect on other projects, etc.

The task of obtaining the approval can be broken down into three elements:

- preparing or amending an investment appraisal to confirm that the project is financially worthwhile;

- obtaining approval to spend the money;

- ensuring that the money is available to spend on the project.

These elements are dealt with below.

5.8.1 Investment Appraisal

Investment Appraisals (IAs) should be prepared for each of the various ways of achieving the objectives. They should include:

- the cost of all staff, contractors and consultants involved, including training costs;

- the purchase price or rent of any necessary hardware, software and consumables;

- the cost of building and any other work;

- the value of all savings and benefits which can be expressed in money terms, or the costs of the system to be replaced;

- the cost of running the system.

Any benefits and penalties which cannot be given a monetary value should be recorded, so that they can be taken into account when taking decisions about the project.

Since the IA is forward looking, assumptions must be made, and recorded, about the likely costs and the likely outcomes of various courses of action, and about areas of risk or uncertainty found. The quality of the assumptions is especially important. Otherwise the result may be production of indifferent data leading to expensive projects being undertaken, or worthwhile projects not being undertaken. The sensitivity of the appraisal must be subjected to analysis of the impact of variations in these areas of uncertainty, using specialist advisers if appropriate.

IA will normally be carried out, with an increasing degree of precision:

- during the Feasibility Study,

- during the Full Study,

- when evaluating tenders,

- during the course of a project if the boundaries or timing change,

- before deciding to go ahead with part only of a project, and so obtain part of the benefit,

- at the post implementation evaluation to ascertain whether the expected savings and benefits have been realised. No special provision will be needed in the budget for this last IA, since it is an appraisal of what has already happened, for comparison with what was intended.

Close control of the project will be needed to contain the costs within the figures used in the IA, and to ensure that the benefits are obtained. To this end, the IA should be checked at the end of each project stage to ensure that it is still valid, before proceeding to the next stage.

The IA process itself consumes resources, and the effort put in should be commensurate with the benefits to be gained from the project, or with the risk involved.

Management and control are covered in Chapter 6 of this guide. Further information can be found in *Guide B4: Appraising Investment in Information Systems.*

5.8.2 Obtaining project approval

Approval is needed at a number of points in the life of the system. At each point, the sum of money to be approved is larger than at the previous point, but fortunately the amount of information available is similarly larger.

The first approval point is during the Strategy Study when the need is perceived for some work to be done. Approval is needed from the ITEC to spend a small amount of money on a Feasibility Study. There may be little information available at this point to justify the work - hence the Feasibility Study - so the case for approval is little more than a statement of the perceived need and the reasons for going further, the particular aspect of the departmental business and IS Strategy which the proposal will support, the likely cost of the Feasibility Study, and confirmation that money is available in the budget.

Although the cost of the Feasibility Study might be relatively low, do bear in mind that one possible outcome is progression to a project costing large sums of money, money which will need to be available in future budgets.

If the Feasibility Study shows that the proposal is worth following up, the study report itself provides the necessary case for progression to the Full Study. The Full Study, in turn, provides information to allow approval to be given (or not) to proceed to the development stages. It is better for the ITEC not to approve progression beyond the Full Study until it has the Full Study report available and is able to see what the cost will be of implementing the proposals.

The above approvals are sought before each project starts; within a project, any approvals to proceed to the next stage will be given by the Project Board, who will seek authority from the ITEC if necessary.

5.8.3   Obtaining financial approval

From the very beginning of the lifecycle (see Chapter 2) and periodically thereafter, it is necessary to ensure that adequate money has been made available in the budget. The cycle for preparing estimates and obtaining approval is long, so some money will have been allocated by the time you arrive on the scene as Project Manager. However, it will almost certainly be spread through several budgets, such as the user's staff budget, the capital budget, and the consultancy budget, as well as the IT staff budget. Appropriate amounts from all sources can be brought together into the project budget.

Each time an investment appraisal is prepared, the opportunity should be taken to ensure that the money needed to cover all the resources (staff, equipment, purchases, consultants etc) required for the project is available. If there is not enough money available, it will be necessary to ask the 'approving authority' whether the provision can be increased.

The approving authority before a project starts will usually be the ITEC. During the course of a project, the first request for approval should be made to the Project Board. If that body does not have sufficient delegated authority it will be necessary to move the request to a higher level. The inherent delay may well lead to changes in the cost or timing of the project, which must be taken into account when framing the recommendation. The Departmental Budgets Officer should be kept informed of all proposals and of any changes to them.

If sufficient money cannot be made available, it will be necessary to examine the IS Strategy to check whether adjustment of priority should be made. Discussions with the proposed user will be necessary to check whether the project should continue at all, or whether it should continue in a reduced form or at a later date. If the project is given greater priority, or is deferred or reduced in scope, the effect on other projects, whether started or not, needs to be checked.

5.9   Assessing the risk to the project

It is useful to you as a Project Manager, and to the Project Board, to assess whether your project is high risk or low risk and, if high, what is the source of the risk. Risk here means the degree of probability that the project will not be completed on time and within the budget. **Its assessment and consideration are in no way a reflection on the Project Manager's competence**, and should not be neglected for that reason. Knowing the degree of risk, and the cause and source of high risk elements, will allow you to direct your efforts where they will be most effective.

What factors, then, affect this probability? They come from four sources: project management, project staff, the nature of the project itself, and the maturity of the departmental management culture.

		Low risk	**High risk**
5.9.1	Project management	Full time, experienced Project Manager.	Inexperienced or part time Project Manager.
		User management is experienced and likely to be active participants.	Inexperienced user management with little participation expected.
5.9.2	Project staff	Users are expected to be of good quality, actively involved and with relevant knowledge of the system.	Little user involvement and little relevant knowledge expected.
		High standard of supervision and narrow span of control.	Span of supervision too wide and level of control inadequate.
		The technical team is experienced, of good quality and with appropriate skills.	Inexperienced team lacking the appropriate skills.
		Staff are dedicated to the project.	Staff have other responsibilities such as systems maintenance.

		Low risk	**High risk**
		Low staff turnover.	High staff turnover.
5.9.3	The nature of the project	Staff are experienced in quality reviews and committed to their use.	No QR programme followed in the past.
		A typical system development cycle, with requirements definition, system specification, systems design etc.	A system development cycle having no formal requirements definition, systems design and build merged etc.
		No unique or new features.	Pioneering, new hardware or software, etc.
		Current main operations will be affected minimally.	Significant impact on mainstream operations.
		Hardware and software requirements determined and documents based on proven standards.	Requirements not documented or not based on proven standards; limited safety margins for contingencies.
		Little or no modification to existing application software.	Extensive modification needed.
		Little or no other development being undertaken concurrently.	Other projects being developed concurrently.
		Little or no dependence on existing or developing systems not under the control of the staff on this project.	Dependent on other facilities not under the control of staff on this project.
		Project duration of one year or less, or small number of work-days compared with other completed projects.	Project duration more than one year, or a large number of work-days.

		Low risk	High risk
		Planning and estimates are based on reliable data.	Planning and estimation data are unreliable.
		Investment appraisal and estimates prepared and well documented, using proven standards.	Approximations used, or estimates not properly documented, or based on unproven standards.
		Suppliers are large, well established companies.	Suppliers are new or one-man businesses.
		Suppliers have a good record for installation, support, delivery etc.	Suppliers' record is poor or unproven.
		Few user departments.	Several user departments.
		The work affects few sites, which are easily accessible to the development team.	Many, or remote, sites are involved.
		Minor impact on user's current or future day-to-day work.	Significant impact on users.
5.9.4	The maturity of the departmental organisation	A well-developed set of standards is in use.	Few standards are used.
		A well-defined quality policy exists.	The quality policy is ill-defined.
		Clear delegation of authority is practised.	Centralised management with little or no delegation.
		Good relationship with departmental Trade Union Side and staff.	Relations with TU side and staff are poor.

5.9.5   The degree of risk

Assessing each of the elements on a scale from low risk to high risk will allow a comparison to be made between projects. Any high risk areas should be drawn to the attention of the Project Board, along with specific proposals to meet the risk. If the assessment suggests that the project is likely to fail, the fact should be drawn strongly to the attention of the Project Board, and to the ITEC.

The degree of risk must be kept under review during the course of the project, to ensure that an area, or indeed a project, which has been classified as low risk does not become high risk without the change being noticed. The risk must be reassessed and reported to the Project Board when seeking approval to progress to the next stage of the project.

5.9.6   Time, cost and risk trade-off

The objective of the Project Manager and the project staff during the planning is to show how the requirement can be delivered as quickly as possible to the required quality with the minimum of work and at the least cost. They must consider alternative ways of achieving the objectives and select the optimum solution.

The objectives when managing a project are slightly different. They are to deliver the specified end-products at the agreed time and within the agreed budget (ie they are constrained by the agreed plan).

The various elements within either of the above objectives do not usually have a direct relationship to each other. Reducing the delivery time may well increase the amount of work which needs to be done and paid for, since using extra staff would increase the cost of management. Reducing the cost may increase the time and effort needed, if the cost reduction means that less experienced staff are used. A large part of the Project Manager's effort will be devoted to reconciling these problems, and assessing the effects of such trade-offs. This assessment is made easier by the planning process (described at 5.3.3) of breaking the work down into smaller components and estimating for each individual component. The effects of each trade-off must be investigated for each feasible combination of components, through all their ramifications of scheduling, management and control, training needs etc, right to the end of the project. This is best done with one of the project management tools or spreadsheets available. Various combinations of skill type and staff levels can be entered, and a rapid calculation of the effect on the investment appraisal obtained. These effects can be noted and compared, and the most desirable, or least objectionable, solution selected. This process is usually known as 'what if?' planning.

5.10   Matrix management and line management

By the very nature of an IS project, the personnel will be drawn from different work areas such as the IT Directorate and one or more user divisions. However, they will be working to a common end, that of producing the project end-product(s). The result will be a mixed organisational arrangement in which the normal vertical hierarchy is overlaid, but not replaced, by an horizontal organisation. This matrix management has its advantages in the form of.

- Greater flexibility in use of resources, because staff can be allocated to the project for short periods, then returned to their 'home' Line Manager.

- Improved information flows because the staff are in a more compact group, leading to better (because more informed) decision making. This is to some extent offset by the slowing down in decision making referred to below.

- Better staff morale and motivation because they are closer to, and can become committed to, the project.

Disadvantages associated with matrix management are as follows.

- The conflict and stress within the organisation which appear to be inevitable, and which can degenerate into personal conflict. This stems from the apparent loss of control of the staff by the 'home' Line Manager, and from problems like approving leave and writing annual confidential reports. These problems may be eased by ensuring that the period during which staff are working on the project, and the tasks to be performed, are clearly defined.

- Decision making may be slowed down (but this may be offset by other factors associated with project management, and in particular by the project management structure which is a part of PRINCE).

- There is often a requirement for additional information. This may be satisfied by ensuring that information produced as part of the project management process is given sufficiently wide circulation.

It is essential that the differences between line and matrix management methods, and the possibility of conflict, are recognised. To reduce the risk of such conflict, the people concerned should be regarded as 'lent' to the project for the period necessary for them to make their contribution. It is essential that.

- The time and period of the loan is well-defined and agreed between the Project Manager and the appropriate Line Manager. This is done by means of the stage plans which schedule the resource usage. During the secondment, staff will be under the control of the Project Manager so far as allocation of work and discipline are concerned, but may well remain under the control of their normal Line Managers for professional standards and annual reporting.

- The tasks to be performed during the loan period (including any technical training) are properly specified. This will be covered by the specification produced during an earlier activity in the project, probably during the Specification or Development stage.

It follows that the plans should be discussed and formally revised if project problems lead to adjustment of the project timing. This is a normal part of management and control of a project anyway.

6 Controlling the project

6.1 What is control?

One definition of management is 'the judicious use of a means to achieve an end'. But what is meant by judicious? How is it done and how do you know that you have done it? The answer is probably best summed up in the word **control.** 'Control' means 'no surprises'. Good control means that estimates are close to reality and when they are not you find out early enough to do something about it.

If you are in control of the variables of a project then you are successfully managing the project. Many managers will say that a successful project is one delivered on time and to budget. Yet rigid control of time and budget may well sacrifice other variables, for example the utility or the quality or the long-term maintainability of the delivered end-product.

6.2 How is control achieved?

Theoretically, the control mechanisms are very simple. All you have to do is plan, or estimate, for the achievement of a particular end-product, to a given quality standard, to achieve a defined utility for a cost which is worthwhile and in a timescale which is acceptable. You then measure progress against those variables, compare the planned achievement with the actual and take any necessary corrective action. The classic control cycle is:

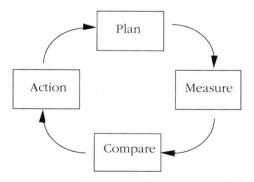

Fig6: The control cycle

An important corollary of the control cycle is that any variable not measured is not controlled.

6.3 What is it important to control?

The question of what is important to control is fundamental to the concept of project management. The reason for using the technique of project management in the first place is that the delivered end-product is important enough to justify the concentration of minds and resources on its development. This implies that resources should be deployed to have the greatest effectiveness in delivering the end-product. Efficiency or the utilization of resources should only be addressed within the context of the project. This implies that you are most concerned with outputs. Tom DeMarco in *Controlling software projects* has estimated that 15% of all projects do not produce anything, but even **that** 15% consumed resources, perhaps in an efficient manner. Projects are unique, risky, important ventures. Therefore measure your output in detail and measure your inputs before they are deployed, ie know the resources at your disposal so that you can produce good estimates and plans. Monitoring outputs will enable close control of the project even if the reasons for divergence from plan are rooted in lack of input resources.

6.4 What are the output variables to control?

The variables which need to be controlled will depend to some extent upon the type of project. However, in most projects the variables which need control are:

- Achievement   - of deliverables against time;

- Quality   - of deliverables;

- Utility   - of the final system;

- Value for money - of the application in business terms.

You will notice that these variables are all outputs and can only be detected **after** the event.

6.4.1   Controlling
         achievement

What is achievement? In IS projects, delivery should only be accepted as having occurred if the end-product has been checked for quality. Typically this would be a peer group review or independent QA Team review where the reviewers sign-off the product as being of a planned quality and planned utility. Measurement is then whether delivered or not, although we can recognise other states eg 'under development', 'ready for quality review' or 'being amended following quality review'.

The worst way to measure achievement is to wait until the end of the project. Unless you break the achievable end-products into smaller, intermediate products the project team is likely to put in the planned number of man-days, and use the planned computer time, budgets and other resources until the planned end-date. Then you are likely to deploy unplanned man-days, unplanned computer time and unplanned budget until the actual end-date.

This problem can be avoided during the planning process by breaking down the final end-product into components which are achievable by one person, carrying out one activity in a duration not less than eight hours and not more than 80 hours. You should set a project standard that no activity in support of an end-product should be planned to take more than 10 working days. You should ask for an interim product even if this makes the overall project take longer. In fact you should reject methodologies and techniques which are not amenable to management and control.

Because the timescale is short, deviation from the plan is easily and quickly detected. Potential project delay and cost overrun are easy to calculate and corrective action can be taken. The task is tedious, but much easier with a support tool.

In order for achievement to be the main measure of control, every activity needs to be directed at, and evidenced by, an end-product, even if it is just a certificate that an activity such as an inspection has taken place.

Planning to this level of detail may be a problem because the details of future activities are dependent upon the results of early activities. This is normal. You should not plan in detail more than six months ahead, but always measure against a detailed plan.

6.4.2	Managing and controlling quality	Variables of achievement are easily identified and measured. Quality on the other hand is frequently difficult to define or measure. Despite this difficulty you are still looking for a binary measurement, ie passed quality review or failed quality review. It is both your measure of quality and your measure of progress.

There are two objectives in controlling quality. They are to ensure first, that the end-product is fit for the purpose, and secondly that it conforms to the standards that the project has adopted.

But how do you know that a product is fit for its purpose? There is an increasing number of tools that can assist in ensuring that their end-products are accurate, complete and consistent, but inevitably this only applies to a proportion of the end-products needed by the project. In general you will need a peer group, or better still an independent opinion, which reviews and confirms the accuracy, completeness, consistency, fitness for purpose and conformance with standards. The review may be formal or informal.

In the informal quality review, the author asks the opinion of his peers. Where the end-product is a document the author might circulate copies and ask for comments. This is a reasonable preliminary, but the Project Manager should insist on a formal quality review for all end-products, where identifiable reviewers meet to discuss and then sign-off the content and quality of the end-product. Such reviews are improved by the presence of an independent reviewer - perhaps a consultant who can report to the Project Board and the Project Manager on the adequacy of the process as well as the specifics of particular end-products.

6.4.3	Controlling utility	The only way to ensure continued utility of end-products is to involve users in the quality assurance and control process. If you do not bother, you will have systems which work perfectly to specification but which are of no use to users because the need has changed and the requirement is consequently different.

Control in this sense means seeking out users and looking for their continued agreement that the end-products are required. However **sometimes the products are technical and are difficult to explain to users.** You should try to explain technical matters in terms of the impact on and usefulness to their businesses. You are looking for binary measurements. Either it continues to be relevant to their needs or not.

6.4.4   Controlling value for money

The value for money of the project was explored in the business case which justified the investment decision.

It is important that the project continues to be viable, but be wary of updating old discounted cash-flow tables. Investment appraisal is intended to inform decisions about future spending. If you wish to decide whether to continue, the same criteria apply. Think only about the **future** investment against the **future** benefits. This can lead to some unlikely decisions. You may have already spent 90% of the project costs and then discovered that the benefits actually achievable are only 50% of the total costs. It may still be worthwhile spending the remaining 10% in order to achieve that 50%. The Project Board will have to explain why they have a system which delivers benefits amounting to only half of the development costs, but a correct decision will have been made.

Probably more significant than value for money is the likelihood of changes in business direction. If they render benefits much smaller, the need to kill what has otherwise been a successful project should not be shirked. It is project management.

The benefits are estimated at times most conveniently aligned with stages of the project. Where delays and cost overruns are experienced impact on benefits should always be identified.

6.4.5   Controlling the unplanned

Perhaps 15% of the resources in any project are spent on unplanned activities. It is the most difficult of variables but if you don't measure it you won't control it. You should find out what the resource is spent on and make sure it is planned in future. This will inevitably involve you in getting people to say what else they do besides planned activities. This leads us into the measurement of resource inputs.

| 6.5 | **Measuring the inputs** | You will also be pressed as a Project Manager to control inputs such as the following. |

- People: numbers
  structures
  turnover
  availability
  skills
  motivation
  productivity.

- Money: budget
  tolerance.

- Materials.

- Other resources, eg computer time or software tools.

Measuring people's effort on particular tasks is generally a good idea. Unfortunately it is one of the most difficult jobs to do, with few rewards for either the measurer or the measured. Measuring people's attendance tends to be fairly easy. Measuring their output can also be fairly easy as we have shown, so measuring productivity in terms of those factors is not difficult. Finding out why there are large disparities in performance is another matter. This involves detailing what people do on an hour-by-hour basis.

Measuring people's effort is best done by observation. Much less reliable information is obtained from getting people to fill out forms and making them account for say 40 hours per week.

The following lists provide some do's and don'ts.

Do:

- make it worth people's while to self-record (if this has to be done) - buy your data with positive feedback;

- get someone other than the person him/herself to measure;

- measure on a sample basis;

- measure in hours against planned tasks;

- allow recording against sub-tasks;

- allow recording against unplanned activities;

- encourage as much detail as possible on unplanned activities;

- collect data at least weekly and preferably daily.

Don't:

- restrict yourself to preset codes;

- insist that it adds up;

- record activities that take less than one hour;

- allow people to submit three months' worth of timesheets at once;

- assess individuals or personal performance from the figures;

- take personnel management action against an individual based on the data given.

People, however honest, will try to anticipate the 'best' acceptable answers and bias their replies accordingly.

Controlling and measuring the contribution of your people resource is probably the most difficult task you have.

6.5.1   How do I know what I've got?

The first problem is in measuring the resource actually made available for the project. You will be asked to work with part-time and shared resources such as database or communications specialists. You will certainly require the part-time services of users.

However, do try to insist that even part-time resources are given on a dedicated basis - for example every Monday or the first Tuesday of the month. If you have to accept resources 'in the margins of time' then ensure that they are not engaged in critical activities.

You should try to find out the degree of continuous concentrated effort likely to be devoted to your project; you should quote only whole hours of uninterrupted work. If this tells you that you have no resources, do not undertake the project. In design and development the 'pick-up' time for any job is likely to be at least 25 minutes, therefore an hour's uninterrupted work is the only unit of effort likely to yield progress.

Staff turnover is a significant variable of availability. Frequent turnover can reduce team effectiveness substantially. In some long projects no-one has been involved throughout. Typically, learning curves are three to four months. The Civil Service tends to lose experienced personnel and recruit trainees and the recovery time for the team will then be of the order of six to nine months.

Having determined availability of staff you need to assess their capability, both skill and productivity, as a team rather than individuals. This is reflected in the gross productivity measures determined from measurement of output compared to gross measures of input. Plans should be reassessed in the light of performance or of efforts made to improve skill or productivity.

You need to know the resources you have in order to plan effectively. Subsequent measurement should be on the outputs and should only occasionally look at the detail of input when there is divergence from plan.

The other inputs of time, money and material are easily identifiable but may still cause problems because of the way such resources are allocated, for example on an annual cycle voted by Parliament. The actual spend should be closely monitored (note 'actual spend' is an input to projects and has no connection with progress).

6.5.2	How are measurement and comparison actually done?

This is a subject of project reporting. There are two main purposes in reporting:

- to convey reassurance about status;

- to show comparison with plans to provide a trigger for decision-making about corrective action.

There are other purposes such as:

- keeping all project personnel aware of progress;

- providing an input assessment;

- providing a basis for charging;

- to give advance warning about problems and issues which will need to be resolved.

6.6 **Reports to and from the project team**

The Project Manager needs to communicate the overall plan to the team and ensure that everyone knows what their tasks are and how they fit in. It is particularly useful if all members of the team can contribute to the production of the project plan.

This should be backed up by task lists issued (say) fortnightly. They can act as turnaround documents on which team members can record their achievement. They can then be input into a tool or technique and compared with the bar-chart for the Project Manager's report of progress against plans. In turn, this reporting should be backed up by documentation of quality achievement from the independent Quality Assurance team.

However, forms do not detect all problems and a regular series of project team meetings should be scheduled so that the manager can detect such intangibles as morale and enthusiasm. In a large project these meetings may have to be structured as team leader meetings and lower level meetings. They should last less than two hours, have a simple agenda, and have simple notes of action required as an output.

6.7 **Reports to the Project Board**

Project Boards tend to be mostly interested in the final delivery date and the total cost. They want to know what has to be done to keep within the acceptable limits of schedule and cost overrun. It is necessary therefore that reports include a projection of future costs and progress.

6.7.1 Earned value graphs and bar-charts

The best graphical illustration is an earned value graph but text will be essential to explain the background to the projection. For a fuller explanation of earned values see Annex E. Earned value graphs tend to be difficult to work out unless there is a supporting tool. A simpler technique is to show progress against plan in a bar-chart. These have the advantage of simplicity but the disadvantage that detail is omitted and progress is difficult to show. (If you sum up major activities on a bar-chart it can easily show all activities in progress. If all the detail is shown, the Project Board has volumes of paper to read.)

On no account should a network diagram be presented to the Project Board as part of a report.

6.7.2	Histograms	Costs can be depicted in comparative histograms or tables as preferred. However, note that these are project inputs and in the context of stable teams are frequently identical from month to month. They are simply a function of the elapsed time of the project.

More useful is a highlight report produced for the Project Board and the Project Manager giving the current status, current problems and future outlook. It should be on a single sheet of A4 paper.

Finally the Project Manager should be asked to account personally for his progress and his proposed future actions to a meeting of the Project Board at intervals in the project.

6.8 What actions can I take?

There is often **nothing** you can do to recover the divergence from plan of an individual end-product. You have produced an estimate; it was wrong. The product will cost more, or take more time, or have less utility than you expected. Projects are unique, risky undertakings. What you **must** assess is:

- the impact of this failure on the final end-product (and if you have followed the advice above it will be a small impact);

- whether the delay or cost overrun or lack of utility is acceptable.

However, in most cases you will be able to take steps to prevent future, similar, activities taking as long by determining the reason for non-delivery and applying resources effectively. For example, if the reason for delay is lack of skill you may wish to recommend a training programme, or employ consultants, or consider whether you should employ someone else.

Options considered should include:

- cancellation - what is the impact of lost benefits and of lost investment,

- reducing the scope of the project - what is the impact on business need and benefits,

- delay - impact on costs.

The important point is a sense of realism. If a project was planned to last twenty months but has taken 16 months to produce the products planned to take ten months, is it really likely that it will only experience some six months' overrun?

6.8.1   Exception plan

If the project deviates from the plan, or shows signs that it is likely to deviate from it, an exception plan will be needed to explain the deviation and to seek approval of the corrective action. The exception plan will be submitted first to the Project Board. If they do not have sufficient delegated authority to approve the proposals it contains, they will pass the report, with their recommendations, to the ITEC for approval.

Corrective action itself requires use of resources and is one reason why the Project Manager needs a limited authority to call upon more resource and why such a call must be strictly justified in his or her plans. This is known as tolerance within PRINCE: it is essential if control is to work.

Senior managers and Project Boards are often reluctant to allow any tolerance, thinking that by imposing a constraint of **no tolerance** they are exercising control. It has the opposite effect in that it prevents the Project Manager from taking any corrective action and the project status can only change in one way, that is a delayed schedule and consequent cost overrun.

7 Managing change

7.1 Success means change

It is in the nature of an organisation to change, particularly if the organisation is a successful one. In fact, the most successful organisations are those which adapt to changing circumstances, or in anticipation of changing circumstances. However, it is essential that all changes proposed are properly evaluated through the Strategy Study and Feasibility Study (see Chapter 2). It is also essential that all changes are properly approved before any project is started, and that changes actually implemented are controlled, because any change will cost money to implement.

If the change is proposed **after** a project has started, its implementation is very likely to delay completion of the project. This will therefore defer the date at which the required benefits will be obtained. You must not try to obstruct change, but if there is no formal mechanism to control changes, the project can quickly go out of control, with delay and extra cost building up until the project eventually delivered bears little resemblance to what has been approved. This is true whether results are measured by end-product specification, or delivery date, or cost. To avoid this situation, a change control procedure should be set up.

In the process of making agreed changes to a project, it will probably be necessary to reschedule the work of the project staff. Since the staff are likely to be taken from a pool of scarce resources, any changes proposed will affect managers of other projects, who will be forced to reschedule **their** projects also. This must be taken into account in any change control procedure.

> Changes can be managed (ie controlled) much more easily if there is a firm foundation of approved plans and specifications, and an infrastructure of procedures, on which to base the management.

| 7.2 | **Why are changes needed?** | The need for change can arise in the following ways. |

a **From within the project**, when it is thought necessary or desirable to make changes to a project already started, eg because someone has thought of another, seemingly better, way of tackling an aspect of the problem, or has thought of new facilities which are considered necessary; or because work done so far suggests that changes are needed.

b **From outside the project**, when new work needs to be done:

- because of changing circumstances, new legislation, etc. This may result in the need for significant change, in which case it is worth considering formal termination of the existing project, and starting afresh with a new project with new details to be approved, planned and controlled in the same way as any other project; or

- because changes to the specification or the timing of another project necessitate changes to this project.

c **After installation of the system**, when minor or major changes are suggested. Again, a procedure needs to be established to record these change proposals and to evaluate them; to recommend whether they should be undertaken by the maintenance team or whether they should be aggregated into a new project; and to obtain approval at the appropriate level.

| 7.3 | **Requests for change within a project** | Within a project of any reasonable size, many requests for change can be generated. Thought should be given to: |

a the way of registering them, and of monitoring their progress until they are incorporated within project plans, or are abandoned; and

b the entries needed in the register to enable monitoring to be done.

Other essentials in a change control system are.

c A definition of what constitutes a change. This can usefully be defined as a change to any item which has been subjected to quality checks and accepted as correct (ie has become a baseline) or has been recorded as a Configuration Item (see also Chapter 5).

d   A clear definition of the method of evaluating the proposed change and its effects on this **and other** projects, and of responsibility for authorising the changes. The effects to be evaluated are:

- the likely effects on other configuration items, or prospective Configuration Items;

- whether staff time can be rescheduled to fit the request;

- the extra cost, or extra time, needed for the project, the latter delaying the release of staff to other projects.

Just as many replanning problems can be caused if staff are rescheduled and released earlier than was originally planned.

e   A way of ensuring that the decision made is recorded and notified to all interested parties and, if appropriate, is implemented in accordance with the approval.

It is desirable to split the responsibility for approval into two parts. Minor changes during the course of a project could be within the authority of the Project Manager to approve, after consultation with the Senior User. Major changes would go to the Project Board, or maybe even higher. In this context, minor changes would be those which did not cause the Project Manager to exceed the limit of his authority (ie his tolerance) and did not amend any item which had been put under configuration control as a baseline. Any other changes would be major. Examples of changes which need approval at a higher level than the Project Board are those which change the boundaries of the project or which take the project cost above the level approved by the ITEC or which affected a project with a different Project Board.

A similar set of procedures could apply to changes proposed after the project has been completed and the project team disbanded. These involve the IT Manager and the maintenance staff, rather than the Project Board and the Project Manager.

Off-specification reports should be dealt with in similar ways. These report where the end-product does not meet the required specification, and it is not intended to alter either of them before the current project ends. However it is preferable to maintain separate registers for each category of report, since different groups of people are involved with each.

7.3.1   The effect on other projects

A major difficulty in evaluating any request for change is to identify exactly whether other projects will be affected by the proposal, and if so which. The problem becomes progressively more difficult as the project progresses and new projects start. These may depend on facilities, eg software, terminals, working practices or local area networks, to be provided by the original project, but which have little impact on the staff of the original project. The same effect can be felt in reverse, of course, when changes or delays in another project start to affect the one you are working on. You then have to adjust your plans, perhaps by revising the specification of end-products, or rescheduling staff, recalculating the investment appraisal and seeking revised financial approval. This problem must be addressed when setting up the change control procedures. It is best resolved as part of a configuration management procedure. This will record all Configuration Items in all projects which are likely to be affected by the change to any particular Configuration Item (see 7.6 for details).

A common problem when changes affect two projects is that one reaps the benefits and wants the change, while the other bears most of the cost and so is resistant to the change. This will be minimised if a proper evaluation of the cost to **all** projects affected is carried out and formally approved at the level of a common Project Board, or higher, as set out above.

7.3.2   When other projects run late

The above covers the situations arising when **prior approval is sought** to change another project. But there will be occasions when another project overruns its scheduled time **without** prior approval, and does not wish to release resources for reallocation to other projects. To ensure that the staff will be available on the date scheduled the Project Manager must keep in touch with the line managers of all staff who will be allocated to his/her project in the near future, whether they are IT staff, user staff or from any other locations. If it is foreseen that staff will not become available then the following should be done:

- negotiate with the manager of the late-running project in an attempt to release the staff on the due date, or

- negotiate a date acceptable to both Project Managers, and

- reschedule either or both of the projects to counter the effects of the delay.

If there is still a problem then the manager of the affected project must report the situation to the Project Board. The report should make recommendations for dealing with the problem, bearing in mind the order of priority allocated to each of the projects. It must include a note of the effect on the investment appraisal. If necessary, the Project Board will refer the matter to the ITEC to arbitrate between the projects. The Project Support Office also has a role to play in monitoring interactions between projects.

The Project Manager must always report to the Project Board if any delay to the project is foreseen.

7.4 Options open to the approving authority

Whatever the reasons for or the nature of the proposed changes, the authorising body will always have three options:

- to give approval to proceed in the timescale proposed (with or without requiring changes to the detail);

- to defer the work until a more suitable time (more suitable because resources are likely to be available then);

- to refuse approval.

7.4 1	Who are the approving authorities?	The approving authorities are likely to be:

The ITEC   if the change will alter the project boundaries, or will affect more than one project with different project boards, or will take the project cost above the approved cost, including contingency sum;

The Project Board   if the request is to change a baselined end-product, or will cause the Project Manager to exceed his contingency sum;

The Project Manager all others.

7.5 Issue management

An issue is defined as a problem which has an effect outside the immediate environment (eg project) where it arose. Examples are where different parts of an organisation approached and solved the same problem in different ways, so that the results were not comparable; or a defect was found in a departmental standard.

Since issues have a widespread effect, it is important that they are resolved quickly.

To resolve an issue the impact of any proposed change must be assessed, eg:

- whether any changes need to be made to existing departmental practices or to existing projects;

- whether future projects will be easier or more difficult to manage and control;

- whether they will become more expensive or take longer to complete;

- the effect on departmental management.

This impact is costed and a report submitted to the issue control authority (usually the ITEC) for a decision. After the decision has been taken, and accepted by all concerned, then of course it needs to be written into departmental instructions.

| 7.6 | **Configuration Management** | During the lifetime of a development project, there will certainly be a number of drafts of any document prepared, and successive versions of any software. Even after the 'final' version of either has been produced, there will be subsequent amendments! This being so, how do the project staff know whether they are working on the current version? And, part of the same problem, how can anyone be certain that two amendments to the current version are not being prepared at the same time, each unknown to the author of the other? The answer is to have a Configuration Management (CM) system whose librarian: |

- gives all Configuration Items (CIs) a unique identification reference;

- records which item(s) lead to its production and which succeed it;

- cross-references to all other CIs which it affects and which are affected by it.

Those cross-references should be independent of project boundaries, so that it is possible to identify CIs in other projects, or elsewhere in the organisation, which might be affected by any changes. Such changes may arise as a result of a request for change, an off-specification report, or reworking in the normal course of project development.

| 7.6.1 | What is Configuration Management (CM)? | CM is a technical discipline intended to make both technical and managerial activities more effective. It provides a focus for the co-ordination of activities where several different people or groups of people are working together. |

Sound CM practices, rigorously applied, offer support to software engineering activities and provide management with much of the information it needs for effective control of all aspects of software product development.

| 7.6.2 | Configuration Items | Configuration Items should be derived from and linked to the product breakdown structure. These are described in section 5.3.3. The CM system should be capable of identifying the current version, restricting the number of copies in circulation and recording who has copies, so that holders can be supplied with revisions as appropriate. |

Once a Configuration Item has been submitted to and logged by the configuration manager, subsequent amendments should not be acted upon until they too have been entered in the log.

Some information about CM support tools is contained in Annex D. A fuller explanation can be found in *Guide B8: Systems Engineering*.

8   Project completion

8.1   Close-down and handover

A project should be formally closed down, and the organisation disbanded, when the project has been completed. It cannot be considered complete until:

- the agreed set of project objectives has been met; and

- all the scheduled end-products have passed the quality review and have been handed over to (and accepted in writing by) the ultimate user and the person who will manage the system: these may, or may not, be the same person.

Quality review procedures should ensure that:

- all the end-products defined as part of the project have been delivered and subjected to quality control and configuration control at the appropriate point in the life of the project;

- all off-specification reports and requests for change have been resolved;

- all trouble reports have been cleared.

It is necessary to ensure before handover that this actually has happened. Also that other items not under the direct control of the Project Manager (eg sub-contracted work and work undertaken elsewhere within the department) have been properly completed; and that Service Level Agreements are in place between the user and the Installation Manager. All of these must be confirmed in the Project Manager's report to the Project Board.

8.1.1   Handover documents

The project documentation should be examined to decide what will be handed over to the various recipients to comply with their requirements. It may be handed over to three recipients:

a   the User - to enable:

- proper use to be made of the facilities provided,
- training of replacement staff;

b   the IT Services Manager - to help them:

- run the system effectively,
- run the system safely ie to ensure the safety of the system and of the personnel,
- maintain and enhance the system in future;

c   the security staff - to enable:

- security to be maintained,
- confirmation that all risk assessment and management matters as well as all security matters have been attended to during development.

Note that the PRINCE manuals specify what system documentation should be produced during the course of the project, how it should be filed and what should be handed over on completion.

One objective of the examinations is to ensure that proper arrangements are made for storing and recording the documentation which is to be retained. Project Board approval should be sought to destroy the rest at an agreed date.

8.1.2	Release of project resources	Project personnel, materials, equipment and any other resources should be formally released to appropriate authorities (Line Managers, equipment store keepers, etc) so that they can be reallocated or costs recovered.

Arrangements should be made for any post-completion support needs such as help-desks, reordering consumable items, and other services. All of these tasks should have been in the project plans from the beginning, but it is as well to check before closing-down the project that they have in fact happened, so that there is a tidy termination.

8.2   **Project evaluation**   A project evaluation should be undertaken as soon as possible after the handover of the developed system, and before formal closedown. Then a report should be submitted by the Project Board to the ITEC. This evaluation should cover:

- whether the scheduled events/timetables were realistic;
- whether the resource estimates were realistic;

- actual performance against planned progress;

- whether management and control procedures were effective and sensible;

- whether the quality system and quality strategy were adequate;

- adherence to standards;

- the usefulness of development tools;

- whether there were any problems with external services;

- reasons for all of the above, if they can be identified.

This information should be collated and analysed to pass on to future projects. If there is a Project Support Office then this is a task for them. If this activity is carried out consistently at the end of every project, a substantial amount of information will be available to be called upon for future projects. It is worth while devising a standard end-of-project review format for this collection and collation of data.

8.3   Post Implementation Review

Arrangements need to be made for the Post Implementation Review to be held six to twelve months after the commencement of live running. This could perhaps use the CCTA's *Method for Evaluating the Impact of Office Systems* (MEVIOS). The review may be conducted by the original development team. However a separate team, including people from IT Services, should be called upon to provide a more objective view in the case of a major installation development, eg the conversion of a total workload from one operating system architecture to another. More detailed guidance on post-implementation evaluation is given in *Guide B4: Appraising Investment in Information Systems*.

Such a review will need the co-operation of, and some contribution from, the executive areas concerned - eg a review of the design of a system should take account of views of the technical specialists concerned. However the review team must make an objective assessment and recommendations. Any proposals for change should be handled under the installation's normal change control procedure.

Typical points to consider during a review are:

- whether the project evaluation report is still valid;

- changes to data volumes and impact on resource requirements;

- quality and accuracy of documentation;

- efficiency of software, job control programs etc;

- use of latest techniques and good practices;

- frequency of failures, reruns etc;

- quality of output and post-processing arrangements;

- customer satisfaction;

- whether the delivered system met the business needs of the user;

- whether the new system was convenient and ergonomically comfortable to use;

- how implementation and operation of the system affected learning time, job satisfaction, productivity, absenteeism/turnover, overall acceptability of the system, etc;

- whether the user training programme was adequate for the users' needs, applied effectively and applied to the right people.

Part C   **Other Considerations**

9   Identifying project problems

9.1   Introduction

It is inevitable that problems will arise during the management of a project. The aim must be to foresee and minimise them, since they will only become more expensive to resolve the later they are found. PRINCE, the government project management method, is designed to show up these problems at the earliest possible moment. This is to allow action to be taken before they become any more troublesome. The most likely areas in which project management problems will arise are:

*   end-products not being delivered as scheduled,

*   quality requirements not being met,

*   resources or other costs overrunning or under-running.

Each of these is considered in more detail below.

9.2   End-products not being delivered as scheduled

This includes end-products being delivered early as well as late. Early delivery is just as likely to be a sign of impending problems. It can indicate that work is being omitted or being done out of the planned sequence, with the result that other end-products will not be available when needed. Or it could show that the estimating was faulty, which will indicate the need to examine the estimates for other end-products, or other projects.

Information is likely to be picked up first through team checkpoint meetings, the results of which are summarised in the Project Manager's highlight report to the Project Board. These checkpoint meetings should draw attention to any need for more, or less, resources than planned, and to tasks which are more complex, or less complex, than was thought at the time the estimate was made. Certainly, the problem of late delivery will show up through delays in arranging the quality reviews. However, the signs of delay are often visible much earlier. If an activity does not start at the scheduled time, then it is unlikely to finish on time. Even if it starts on time, delays are inevitable if resources cannot be applied to the task at the time and in the quantity scheduled.

It may be that the agreed resources are being used at the time scheduled, but the particular end-product is not progressing according to the plans. Is this because the task is proving more difficult than expected? Or is the effort in fact being put into another end-product, and maybe even into one that has not yet been approved under the change control procedure?

9.3 **Quality requirements not being met**

This is a difficult problem to foresee, and may well emerge only when an end-product fails to pass the quality review, or if the team leader is reluctant to submit it for its quality review. Informal quality reviews during the course of production can help identify the problem at an early stage. Similarly it can be helpful to break work down into production of small end-products, each of which can be subject to quality review when completed. The cost of the reviews necessary to find the problem earlier should be balanced against the risk and the cost of delay if the problem is found later. Possible causes of failure to meet the quality requirements are:

- use of team members with lower levels of skill and experience than was expected when the schedules were prepared;

- work being done on unplanned tasks, resulting in less time being available to build the necessary quality into the planned end-product;

- the quality requirement was inadequately specified;

- the specification asked for a standard higher than appeared necessary to the project staff, so that there was no commitment to produce the end-product to the standard specified.

If the end-product does not meet the specification, the problem is normally resolved immediately, by requiring a change to the end-product. This will involve a delay to the project. There will be infrequent occasions, however, when it may be impossible to make changes and the situation must be accepted. In such circumstances, an off-specification report should be raised and attached to the quality review report. The off-specification report should explain:

- the extent of the fault;

- the reason it occurred;

- its effect on the specification, timing and cost of this and any other project;

- the reason why acceptance of the situation is recommended.

This must then be submitted for acceptance by all user divisions who may be affected. If it is accepted then it must be reported to the Project Board.

If the end-product meets the specification, but does not work, or does not produce the desired effect; or if an error is discovered after unit testing has been completed then a project issue report must be raised and the problem must be resolved in a similar way.

Both the off-specification report and the project issue report should be treated as a request for a major change, since either will result in a change to an agreed baseline document. The submission to the Project Board should, if appropriate, be accompanied by an exception report, detailing all proposed changes to the project and stage plans.

9.4 Resources or other costs over- or under-running

This is picked up through the regular (weekly or fortnightly) returns of effort expended and progress made. The figures of effort and progress should be compared with each other, and with what was planned, and investigated if they do not match.

9.5 Wider problems

Some problems will have an effect across a whole range of projects, or a large part of a department. An example is when a defect is found in a departmental standard. Such occurrences are usually called 'issues', and are dealt with under 'Issue management' in section 7.5.

10   Different project types

10.1   Introduction

The majority of this guide is concerned with general matters applicable to most, if not all, projects. However, projects come in many guises and the basic structure will need to be modified to meet the needs of specific types of project. Information may be found in the PRINCE documentation, in addition to that set out here.

10.2   How many projects?

At the highest level, both the formulation of a Department's IS Strategy and the implementation of that strategy can be controlled as projects. Within the Strategy, individual elements of the IS lifecycle such as:

- Feasibility Study,

- Full Study,

- physical system design and development, and

- procurement

can be treated as separate projects.

The way in which elements of the lifecycle are resourced and achieved varies. There is a progression from utilising entirely in-house resources through limited use of consultancy services to turnkey projects and full facilities management of IS services. Each of these types of project is managed in a slightly different way, as described below. However, all projects will commence with an initiation stage to define the project scope and to set up the organisation, control procedures and quality review procedures.

10.3   IS Strategy

The strategy planning process consists of an Initial Study (to establish the baseline); annual reviews (to build incrementally); and major reviews (to cope with significant change).

The Initial Study is a significant exercise and most departments will set up a special study team, using external consultants to augment departmental skills and resources. The duration, numbers and skill mix required for a Strategy Study will vary according to the size of the organisation under review; the scope and depth of the study; and what has gone before. The strategy planning project establishes the study teams and defines responsibilities for all team members, including those of involved senior management.

The IS Steering Committee will act as the Project Board during the different stages of initial study, review and implementation, but the **roles** may be different from the usual PRINCE roles. The review and implementation stages will on occasions run concurrently.

For more information see *Guide A2: Strategic Planning for Information Systems.*

10.4 Feasibility Study

The major end-product of the Feasibility Study is the Feasibility Study Report. The findings of this report have an impact on any succeeding development project. It is therefore important that all interested bodies are fully involved in the project organisation and that a measure of agreement is reached about the general direction of the project. It is particularly important that the user roles on the Project Board and Project Assurance Team (see Chapter 3) are filled with care and that informed technical advice is available on these two bodies.

The Project Manager is normally appointed from the client or user area. Because much of the work in a feasibility study is investigative, involving many interviews and much assimilation of data, estimating effort and planning timescales can reasonably be based on past experience. Standard change control procedures are not implemented at this point in the lifecycle.

For more information see *Guide B2: The Feasibility Study.*

10.5 Full Study

Often the Full Study is a natural progression from a Feasibility Study. If this is the case then the plans for both the full study and for the initiation stage should be drawn up towards the end of the Feasibility Study.

The project organisation will vary slightly according to the solution being investigated. However it is desirable to retain the same or similar people in the project organisation for the Feasibility Study, the Full Study and the development project whenever possible. Examples of the variations and information about stages are given in the *PRINCE Subject Guide on the Full Study.* End-products will vary according to the solution being considered. Change control procedures will be introduced during the specification stage of the Full Study.

After the submission of the Full Study Report, there may be a long interval whilst submissions are made to bodies other than the approving authority. The project may go into a period of suspension during the approval process and allowance must be made for this in the project plan and the design stage plan.

For more information see *Guide B3: The Full Study.*

10.6   In-house development

Considerable effort will be needed for resourcing, planning and controlling an in-house development. In some cases the choice of staff will be restricted by the needs of other projects. Within that limitation, the project size and duration will determine both the management organisation and the make up of the development teams. These in turn will impact on the formality of the reporting methods. Thus, in large projects there may be more levels of organisation, controls and reporting, or a wider span of control, making it necessary to have more formal methods in place. While the IT Directorate should find such formal controls commonplace, this is unlikely to be so with users, who will need training in the method of control.

There may be a conflict to be resolved between the merits of using one of the more competent members of the IT Directorate as Technical Assurance Co-ordinator (TAC) or of keeping that individual as a team leader or team member. Remember, however, that the TAC acts as a consultant on quality matters, and so is able to raise the standard of the whole project.

When the whole of the IS project lifecycle (Feasibility Study, Full Study and development) is carried out in-house the same Project Board and Project Assurance Team should be retained throughout.

10.7   Turnkey projects

A turnkey supplier may undertake the day-to-day management and control of the design, development and testing. This does not remove the department's overall responsibility for the management and control of the project. Technical skills are still likely to be needed, within the department, especially if plans need modification during the procurement stage of the project. This applies particularly to projects involving technical design studies. The department will still need a project organisation, with the supplier providing the technically skilled resources.

The technical roles on both the Project Board and project assurance team may be the most difficult to fill. It may therefore be necessary to employ an independent consultant to assist with, or undertake, the Technical Assurance Co-ordinator role.

Throughout the turnkey procurement process it is important that suppliers are made aware of the requirements that the use of PRINCE will impose upon them. The requirement for the contractor to use PRINCE methods, and the level of involvement in PRINCE procedures should be agreed in both the Memorandum Of Agreement and contract. There are two aspects of reporting to be considered: the internal departmental structure; and the supplier to department structure. The latter may vary according to the supplier's practice of appointing either an account manager or a technical manager to act as the interface with the departmental project organisation.

Change control procedures need special attention since changes may provide the opportunity for a supplier to increase the contract price; the difference between changes to requirement and changes to contract, including overlaps, must be clearly defined.

For more information see *Guide E3: Turnkey Projects.*

10.8   Consultancy Study

If consultants are employed to do a study then changes to the normal project organisation may be necessary. One of the senior consultants may be required to have a role within this organisation. The senior technical role on the Project Board is, however, not the best position for this person, since his or her objectives will be different from the department's. A departmental manager should be appointed to oversee the work of the consultancy team, which will work to its own manager or team leader. The responsibilities of these two people and reporting procedures to be employed between them need to be clearly defined before the project commences.

The use of consultancy services will typically be in the situation of a shortage of qualified staff within the department. In these circumstances it may be advisable to employ further independent assistance for technical assurance and quality assurance. Terms of reference should be as definitive as possible. The specification for the work will provide a basis for planning the project and setting controls.

For more information see *Guide E2: The Hire and Management of Consultants.*

10.9	**Procurement**	Procurement is the process of acquiring goods and/or services which commences with the issue of a requirement and ends when the supplier of the goods and services has been paid in full for delivery of acceptable products, or for the satisfactory completion of work. Procurement can form a project in its own right in cases such as replacement of hardware or bureau equipment. Alternatively it may be one of the stages, or part of several stages, in an in-house development, turnkey or consultancy study project.

In most cases the project organisation will be the same as for any other model. The exceptions will involve the straight purchase of replacement hardware, when the IT Directorate can be regarded as the user. In addition where bureau services are involved there will be the need for a customer/client liaison group. Hardware and software procurement projects will normally have four stages; Initiation, Study/Requirement, Procurement and Installation. For more information see *Guide B6: Procurement*.

10.10	**Facilities Management**	Facilities Management (FM) is the provision of an on-going service by an external agency. This could include machine facilities and accommodation; management and support; software development and maintenance; hardware and software acquisition. Management by the client department will be at two levels.

a Development of new systems and enhancement of existing systems. The client department will establish a PRINCE organisation to **procure** the FM arrangement and from time to time may need additional project organisations for new developments. It is likely that a senior manager from the FM contractor will attend Project Board meetings in a non-executive role, in addition to the client department Project Manager. Quality of service can be assured by a combination of audits by the contractor and independent specialists. The contractor should be required to use PRINCE. This will facilitate monitoring and change control.

b Management of the overall FM arrangement including continual liaison to ensure that the service levels of the day to day arrangement are adhered to. The PRINCE project management techniques (as used for development) are not appropriate for management of FM arrangements after they have been procured.

For more information see *Guide E4: Facilities Management*.

10.11 Conclusion

We hope that you have found this guide useful and informative, and that it will help you complete all your projects on time, to budget, and with all the required functions and quality.

The index is intended to help you come back and dip into the guide to refresh your memory as particular problems arise. There is a bibliography with a list of some useful books if you want to look at particular aspects in greater depth. The glossary provides a quick reference to the various terms peculiar to project management, and to special meanings of other terms.

Annexes

A   PRINCE overview

A.1   PRINCE: the standard project management method

PROMPT was adopted by central government as a framework within which a project could be correctly specified, designed and implemented. Following a period of development and enhancement of the central government version, its name was changed to PRINCE, in recognition of the differences which exist between the versions in use in the private sector and in government.

Although PRINCE covers all aspects of IS project management, it is applied only at the level required to satisfy the particular need. The appropriate level of control is established by the Project Board at the time the project is initiated, by:

- defining the project and selecting the number of stages required,

- defining the frequency of control points and reporting, and

- setting the control tolerance to be allowed.

For all projects, the framework and the terminology is the same.

A.2   Defining the project

PRINCE helps ensure that a project is fully defined and scoped, by using Product Breakdown Structures (see Fig A1) to identify all necessary products, whether they are to be produced within the product, already exist or are to be produced by another project.

At the top of the structure is the **system** (or report, etc) which the project has been commissioned to produce. Products are grouped into three sets - management, technical and quality products - reflecting both the PRINCE distinction between management and technical activities and the need for the quality control to be independently auditable.

PRINCE illustrates the major products of a model IS project and shows the initial levels of the standard product structure (an inverted tree). In this way the model of the whole project is always complete, but the level of detail increases as the project progresses.

Fig A1: Product breakdown structure

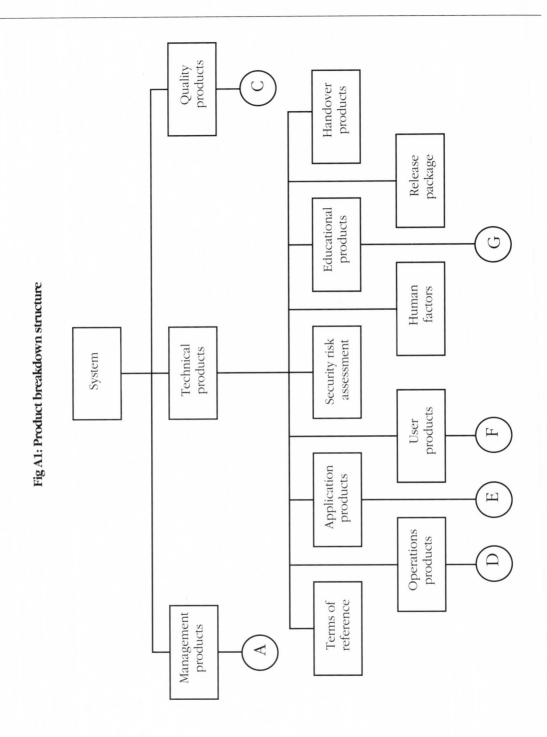

First of all, the standard models enable the Project Board to focus on what the project has to **deliver** - not the same as what it has to **do.** Secondly the models enable the Project Board to identify things they **don't** have to deliver - either something not needed; or which already exists; or which someone else is providing. In the latter case, a contact point with another project is identified. Thirdly, the products can be described with ever-increasing accuracy, and most importantly the specific qualities and quality attributes for a product can be identified, documented and subsequently tested for.

Once the products have been determined, the activities necessary to produce them can be identified.

A.3   Stages

A PRINCE project is divided into stages. Each stage ends at a key point, where a formal decision must be taken whether to proceed to the next stage, or to abandon (or defer) the project. Such a key point might be where tenders are received, and acceptance of one of them will introduce a new set of circumstances and new commitments. There must be at least two stages, covering project planning and then implementation of the plan, but there may be five to seven stages depending on the type of project. Typical stages are set out below, but the actual number of stages are determined during the planning process. Each stage has its own characteristic end-products. The production of these end-products to the agreed standard precedes the formal termination of a stage.

A.3.1   Initiation Stage

The purpose is to prepare a more detailed project specification for approval by the Project Board. This is delivered as a Project Initiation Document which also defines:

- objectives and timescale of the project,

- the management organisation and major control points for all stages,

- the resources allocated,

- project quality criteria, and

- tolerance for all stages.

It also identifies risks to successful completion of the project.

		It includes project resource and technical plans (see Chapter 5) in sufficient detail to calculate and allocate costs and resources for the project.

A.3.2   Specification Stage   During this stage detailed user specifications and user acceptance criteria are produced. User education, data conversion and system installation strategies are defined.

A.3.3   Logical Design Stage   During this stage a detailed definition of the logical data structure and the content of each component are produced from the user specification. Individual processes are specified in detail. The end-products are a composite logical data design and detailed process outlines.

A.3.4   Physical Design Stage   This is concerned with the conversion of the logical design to a physical design suitable for implementation in a particular hardware/software environment, refined to meet performance requirements and specified in detail. The end-products are:

- database/file specifications,
- program specifications,
- system test plans.

A.3.5   Development Stage   The main activities are to design, write and test procedures and programs; to produce the following end-products:

- programs and procedures,
- completed system manual,
- education and training manual,

and to conduct a comprehensive test of the whole system.

A.3.6   Installation Stage   The objectives of this stage are to prepare the operating environment to accept the new system, to install it and to carry out any data conversion and clean-up work found necessary. User acceptance tests are performed against the criteria specified in the specification stage. The installation stage ends when the new system is ready for operational use. The end-product is a user-accepted system.

A.3.7   Operation Stage   The main objectives of this stage are to monitor and improve system performance during the system's early operational life, verify system update and recovery procedures and resolve any failure to meet user and technical specifications that may have been discovered during installation. The project is terminated by a formal transfer from project management to the Service Manager. The end-product is a fully operational and maintainable system.

A.4   PRINCE components   Each PRINCE stage has five components. They are:

- Organisation

- Plans

- Controls

- End-products

- Activities.

The last two are covered above at A.2, the others are detailed below.

Each of the PRINCE components is supported by documentation which includes descriptions, checklists, model job descriptions, objectives, standard planning formats and procedures, together with recommended techniques to support the Project Manager and Stage Managers and their staff.

A.5   Organisation   PRINCE requires the establishment of the following.

A.5.1   Project Board   The Project Board is appointed to manage the project for its whole duration. It consists of three senior management responsibilities, each representing major project interests, namely:

Executive (Chairman)	Appointed by the ITEC to provide overall departmental guidance and assessment throughout the project development cycle.
Senior User	Representing the business area and all users of the system.

107

	Senior Technical	Representing areas which have responsibility for technical aspects of the project.

A.5.2   The Project Assurance Team

This is appointed for the duration of the project. The members of the team have three technical and administrative responsibilities. They are:

- Business Assurance Co-ordination to maintain administrative assurance controls;

- Technical Assurance Co-ordination to maintain technical assurance controls;

- User Assurance Co-ordination to represent business and other user interests and to maintain user assurance controls.

These activities cross the stage boundaries, and maintain the continuity of project development activities and the integrity of end-products.

The Project Manager and Stage Manager roles are assigned to individuals in accordance with the needs of the project. One individual may be appointed to both roles, which means that he/she performs both sets of tasks. Guidance is given on how to decide what is appropriate and on how the duties should be allocated.

A.5.3   Project Management roles

A **Project Manager** is appointed for the duration of the project, to plan the project and define responsibilities for each stage manager. Thereafter, he ensures that the project progresses to time and budget, reporting to the Project Board and initiating any corrective action as necessary.

A **Stage Manager** is appointed for each stage and is given the task of ensuring that stage end-products are produced on schedule to acceptable standards and within budget. The Stage Manager is supported by the stage team(s) responsible for producing the end-products of the stage. At the discretion of the Project Board the same person may manage more than one stage and, in some cases, the entire project.

Teams are created during each stage to implement the project. The team organisation, responsibility definitions and the allocation of these responsibilities to individuals will depend upon the size and nature of the project and the skill mixes available.

A.6   Planning

PRINCE requires a structured set of management and technical plans to achieve effective managerial and technical control of a project. There are three types of plan and up to four levels.

A.6.1   Resource Plans

The resource plans are used to identify the type, amount and period of use of the various resources required during the project cycle.

The Project Resource Plan is mandatory for all projects. It is a top-level resource plan produced by the Initiation Stage team to quantify the resources needed for succeeding stages of the project.

The Stage Resource Plan contains details of all required resources for a stage. It may be produced at two levels of detail: the first in summary form for approval by the Project Board; the second in more detail for the Stage Manager and against which actuals are recorded. It is prepared before the stage commences, in time for submission to the End Stage Assessment meeting of the previous stage.

The Detailed Resource Plans are created as necessary to plan the required resources for a particular activity (eg Systems Test).

A.6.2   Technical Plans

Technical Plans (in the form of a bar chart) are used:

- to identify the sequence of events,

- to define timescales, and

- to assign responsibilities for producing end-products.

	The Project Technical Plan	is mandatory for all projects. It is produced during the Initiation Stage to show the major activities that will occur during system development. It is a top-level plan produced in conjunction with the Project Resource Plan. Both the Project Resource Plan and Project Technical Plan form main end-products of the Initiation Stage.
	Stage Technical Plan	is prepared for each stage of the project and shows all technical activities to be performed within that stage. The Stage Technical Plan is produced at the same time as, and to complement, the Stage Resource Plan.
	Detailed Technical Plans	will probably be necessary in all but the smallest projects. They are used to detail further major activities (eg System Test) and may be specific to a particular stage or may cross stage boundaries.
	Individual Work Plan(s)	are produced as necessary from the Stage and Detailed Technical Plans to allocate detailed activities to specific people within a stage team. Actual progress is reported against these plans for later compilation of control reports.
A.6.3 Exception Plan	**The Exception Plan**	is required only when a deviation from the plans in terms of actual cost or time has exceeded or will exceed tolerances previously defined by the Project Board. It shows the action proposed to meet the deviation.

A.7	**Controls**	PRINCE provides a control structure to be applied during each stage. The control components cover all aspects of project activity and allow the Project Board to assess project status before committing the Department to further expenditure and/or a revised timescale. Controls are applied via meetings of project management and project staff as required, each meeting producing a set of predefined documents. There are four types of control meetings supplemented by comprehensive reporting and change control procedures.
A.7.1	The End Stage Assessment (ESA)	This is a mandatory management control. It occurs at the end of each stage. It consists of a formal presentation by the Project Manager to the Project Board of the current project status and also requests approval of the Resource and Technical plans for the next stage. Approval by the Project Board is needed at an ESA before the project can proceed to the next stage.
A.7.2	The Mid Stage Assessment (MSA)	This is an optional management control. It may be held for one of the following reasons.

- As an interim control point for the Project Manager and/or Project Board.

- As a formal Project Board review part-way through a stage.

- To authorise work to begin on the next stage before the current one is complete.

- As the mechanism for approving Exception Plans.

- To make decisions about the project when unplanned situations arise.

A.7.3	The Checkpoint Meeting	This is a periodic technical and management control point. It is conducted by the Stage Manager, or by the Project Assurance Team on his behalf, and provides the base information used to update actual achievement against that planned on stage technical and resource plans.
A.7.4	The Quality Review	The Quality Review is a technical and management process which is exercised on all end-products.

A.8 **PRINCE documentation**

PRINCE is structured into three levels documentation of each with a precise purpose and aimed at a particular audience.

The Introduction to PRINCE describes the concepts and structure of the methodology giving 'what to do' information.

The Management, Technical and Quality Guides provide detailed 'how to do it' guidance.

The system file, stage files and quality files form an up-to-date record of progress as it occurs - the 'where to file it' information. These documents give full details of PRINCE.

B   Project management support tools

**B.1   The need for
support tools**

Although more than a computer and project management
software are required to manage IT projects effectively,
there is little doubt about the impact that software tools
have had in improving IS project management. Many tasks
in planning and control were not done, or only partially
done, prior to the introduction of project management
software, mainly because of the complexity and difficulty of
setting up the plan initially and then updating it. If the
project went seriously wrong, it became almost impossible
to re-plan in a realistic timescale.

Initially the tools were expensive and required dedicated
machines. They were therefore used only on very large
projects. Indeed, tools running in mini- or mainframe-
based multi-user, multi-access environments are still
required for some large projects or groups of projects. The
advent of low-cost microcomputer tools means that a lot of
the benefits gained on larger projects are now available to
medium and even small projects. However, the quality of
the microcomputer tools is somewhat variable, especially in
the control areas of project management. This Annex will
therefore not give a comparison of tools as this is a rapidly
expanding market. Instead, it will look at what should be in
a tool to support project management.

B.2   User interface

When appraising a project management support tool, you
should look for the following.

- Logically structured and easy-to-use menu systems.

- Good help and error trapping. Help should be
context sensitive and error messages should not
send the user searching manuals for the meaning of
error codes. The help and error messages should
direct the next course of action.

- Rapid access to each screen or window.

- The use of batching functions for data input,
processing and output. They can be big time-savers.

- Systems that support transport of data to and from
the package. They too can be another big time-
saver.

- Clean, consistent exits and quits from each function.

You should avoid:

- unnecessary gimmicks like sound, or a badly integrated mouse operation;

- cluttered screens and over-use of colour and windows.

B.3   Features necessary for planning

Beware of systems that allow the manager to 'Manage as has always been done'. Frequently, one of the reasons for buying a package is to avoid just that.

The package should support the project management method used by the department. In particular, avoid products that are contrary to any critical attribute of a method.

Ensure that the package supports the activity networking method used by the department. The two most common are Precedence (also known as activity-on-the-node) and Arrow (often called IJ or activity-on-the-arrow).

Ensure that the package will allow entry of all relevant project related data especially activities, durations, resources (people and money) and products.

The package should be able to undertake:

- a straight time analysis (resource overloads ignored),

- a time-limited schedule (end-date is sacrosanct and activities are moved within float to reduce overloads), and

- resource limited schedule (resource limit is absolute, activities are delayed until resources are available within limitations).

More sophisticated packages permit greater 'tweaking' of the schedule.

Useful features include support for 'what-if' processing, easy archiving, comparison of plan options, 'quick and dirty' reports rather than only high-quality plots. The product should support top-down planning. More sophisticated packages should offer modelling support, resource scheduling and management across a number of projects.

In 'selling' the project plan to management, high quality reports are a must. Plotting, the use of colour and high resolution graphics are all useful.

The ability to 'baseline' the plan for comparing planned with actuals during control.

B.4 Features required for control

These are as follows.

- The ability to baseline the plan and not subsequently overwrite the plan dates when entering actuals.

- The ability to add/delete and modify data without affecting the integrity of the baseline plan.

- Reporting of progress at various levels depending on the end-user of the data. The idea of one page project summaries should be supported especially for senior management.

- Exception reporting (eg a report showing activities that are late, not just all activities).

- The ability to re-plan the remainder of the project (and re-baseline) if things go seriously wrong without affecting the integrity of historical data.

Forecasting and trend analysis are useful features.

During the control cycle reports should compare planned against actuals/forecast wherever appropriate. The input of actuals should be consistent with the methodology being used. If another system (eg effort recording) collects the actual data, facilities should exist to transfer the data and so avoid unnecessary retyping.

The Project Manager 'owns' the plan. Facilities should not exist which allow, for example, a team leader to update the plan without the Project Manager's approval. This is especially applicable in multi-user multi-access environments.

B.5 Types of package available

Packages broadly fall into four areas ranging in cost from roughly £100 at the bottom end of the PC range to £500,000 or more for dedicated mini- and mainframe versions.

B.5.1	Low-price/low functionality	In general products at he low priced end of the market are easy to use, 'black box', good on planning but poor on control packages. They are characterised by a limited number of activities; little or no updating capability; and limited sorting and selection of data. But they are cheap, they work on minimum configuration hardware and are better than nothing.
B.5.2	Mid-price/reasonable functionality	Packages in the next price bracket offer a fair bit more. They are still black box, but the updating and control features are stronger and frequently include such features as report writers and on-screen plan composition. The purchasing decision will depend on the applicability to the project management methodology especially in the project control area.
B.5.3	Higher priced PC products/high functionality	The next level is the top-end personal computer (PC) market. These products are often linked to a database. At the basic level they use a 'language' rather than menu selection and allow applications to be built or modified using the language to support the departments methodologies and practices. Limits above 50,000 activities are not uncommon at this price level. They offer many of the features of much more expensive mini-and mainframe products and the more sophisticated products offer multi-user and multi-access capabilities with appropriate hardware. However, they are more expensive not just in terms of software costs but also hardware and training but they do offer the prospect of larger benefits.
B.5.4	High-priced mini- and mainframe based	Above the PC packages are the mini- and mainframe based products. These are usually linked to a database and often to other mainframe-based products. They are also much more of a departmental tool rather than strictly a project management tool. Some can offer features such as Document and Budgetary Control and frequently have risk analysis packages. The user interface is usually more primitive than micro based packages but the gap is closing. They offer speed, size-limit and integration advantages over the top-end micro packages and generally have better and more sophisticated scheduling facilities.

> Warning : 'Easy to Use' can mean for some packages 'Easy to Misuse', at some peril to the project.

C   Planning and control diagrams

C.1	**Introduction**	Chapter 5 suggests various techniques which can be used to plan and control a project, and includes examples of diagrams. More information on these techniques is set out in this annex.

C.2   Project networks

A project network can run to many hundreds of activities. The difficulties of drawing it in the first place and of making subsequent amendments mean that it is best prepared using one of the many computer packages on the market (especially if the package is part of a project support tool). The tasks of drawing and amending can be simplified by the judicious combination of activities to make larger groups, as is done in higher levels of the work breakdown structure.

As well as assisting the Project Manager to gain an overall view of the project, a network can assist at specific points in the life of a project. For example, it can show conveniently the interrelationships involved when planning the testing of a suite of programs.

C.3   Gantt chart

A Gantt chart (developed around 1917 by Henry L Gantt) shows planned activities and actual progress by means of horizontal bars set against a time scale.

The chart can easily be kept up-to-date as work progresses, and can be amended to accommodate a few changes. If amendments become too numerous, a new chart will need to be produced: the advantage of a Gantt chart is that it can be produced easily on most types of printer (character, dot matrix or graphics) and can be copied easily if the symbols are carefully chosen to reproduce in black and white. It is worth emphasising here that **any amendment or redrawing must not hide or disguise the originally agreed plan**. This **must** be preserved (and continue to be shown) to act as a baseline for comparison with all future versions, so that the sum of all the changes can be seen. The alternative is to risk a gradual, and unnoticed, drift of time and/or cost until (to everyone's surprise) the product eventually delivered (even if **exactly** in accordance with the current plan) bears no resemblance to what was first planned.

| C.4 | **Resource plans** | Resource plans show all the resources (own staff, consultant's or agency staff, computer time, hardware or software purchases etc) required for all the activities to be undertaken, set against a time scale, and complement the technical plan. It is well to start with staff numbers and grades, then convert to money and add in non-staff costs. There must be room to show actual use of resources alongside the planned usage. There should be a cumulative total of planned use and actual use, for ease of comparison and control. |

| C.5 | **Resource loading** | The resource plan may be summarised into a histogram resource loading histogram or into a graph (x axis = time; y axis = cost) to compare planned and actual expenditure, with the contingency limits indicated. |

| C.6 | **End-product lists** | End-product lists show all end-products to be delivered during the stage, arranged in order of delivery date, with space to enter: |

- date due for delivery,

- date ready for the quality review,

- date passed the quality review.

Comparison of the date due with the current date and with the date the quality review was completed will give a ready indication of progress to date.

| C.7 | **Responsibility lists** | There are parts of projects, particularly around the implementation stage, where the responsibility for carrying out particular tasks is not very clear. Examples of such tasks might be preparing test data, converting files, ordering equipment or consumable stores. The responsibility will be clarified if the Project Manager prepares a list of such tasks and of those who have accepted responsibility for carrying them out. These tasks will be reasonably uniform from project to project, so a standard responsibility checklist can be developed, and will reduce the chance of overlooking any of the tasks. |

Fig C A Resource Loading Histogram

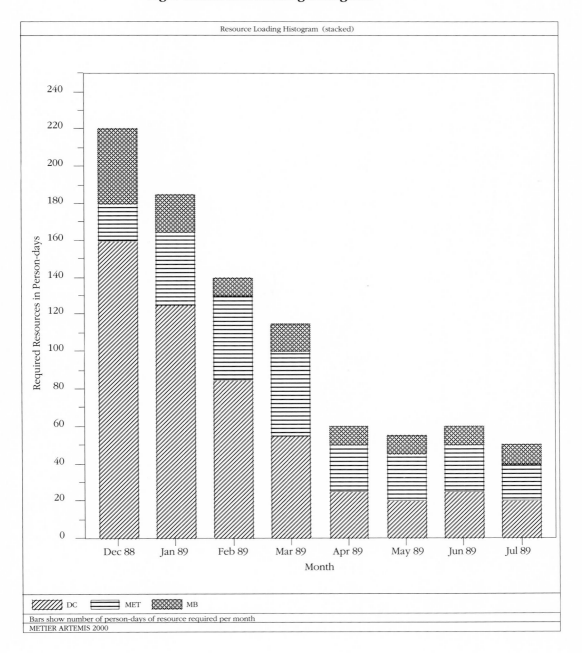

D   Configuration Management support tools

D.1   Categories of tools

Configuration Management (CM) support tools fall into two broad categories.

- Tools which hold information about Configuration Items.

- Tools which in addition to the above hold and provide access control over all representations of the Configuration Items.

Tools in the first category obviously have far less functionality than tools in the second category and consequently tend to cost considerably less. They can often be run on personal computers. Tools of the second category tend to require larger machines and should ideally run on the development hardware and under the development operating system.

D.2   Existing tools

Most CM tools have been developed with military systems in mind, where the software is embedded in the hardware (as ROMs) rather than loaded in from (eg) a floppy disc. Most are not **ideally** suited to information technology systems although some could be used by ignoring some of the functionality. Usually this would be like using a sledge hammer to crack a nut.

E   Earned value

E.1   Introduction

Earned Value is a measure widely used in engineering projects to put a figure on 'real' technical achievement and enable comparison with planned achievement. It can be used as the basis for payment profiles, and contrasts with the measurement of actual resource usage compared with planned usage. In fact the two measures are related in that expenditure on resources cannot cease until all activities and end-products are complete. It follows that if you can predict when all end-products will be complete then you should be able to predict the total project cost.

It is frequently the case that tasks or projects are allocated to teams of fixed size and thus comparing resource allocation with resource actuals is not very useful.

E.2   Calculation of earned value

Earned value is calculated by allocating a 'value' to every activity or end-product - before the project starts. As end-products are completed, its allocated value is accrued until all end-products have been completed and the maximum earned value has been reached, ie the project has ended.

The earned value of an end-product is not related directly to the cost of the resources expended producing it. Thus if a value of £1000 was assigned to an end-product, it could cost £2000 to produce but would still only accrue £1000 value on delivery.

E.2.1   Deciding on the value to be used

There are a number of alternatives when deciding on the value of an end-product but the easiest figure to use is the original budgeted estimate of the cost of producing each end-product. **The sum of the estimates for the individual end-products is the maximum earned value. This contrasts with the total estimated project cost which is the total of the estimated costs of resources made available to the project.** Because of dependencies between activities and their required resources it is never possible to utilize available resources completely and thus maximum earned value will usually be lower than the total estimated project cost. This is **not** bad planning but represents the degree of flexibility in a project.

E.3   **When should value accrue?**

There are a variety of opinions about when value accrues. Some formulae include the percentage complete of unfinished activities. However the PRINCE methodology suggests that progress should only be counted when end-products have been quality reviewed and signed off, and that planning should be sufficiently detailed to ensure that no activity is longer than two weeks. This gives a cumulative value line on a graph which is stepped in value every two weeks.

E.4   **Use of earned value**

By comparing the actual earned value 'curve' with the planned line, and then projecting it either logically using a network or statistically using the trend, the delivery date of the last end-product can be predicted ie the end of the project. By extrapolating the costs of resources available until this date the total project cost can be predicted. All this can be represented on a graph - see Figure E1.

E.5   **Summary**

In summary the earned value graph is a one page snapshot of the cost and schedule status of a project with predictions of the final end-date and total project cost. The PRINCE tolerance controls can be superimposed giving a Project Board early warning of likely delay and cost overrun.

The calculation involved would be very tedious to do manually on a regular basis and earned value is rarely a feature of manual systems. The CCTA product ADEPT produces an earned value graph as a standard report.

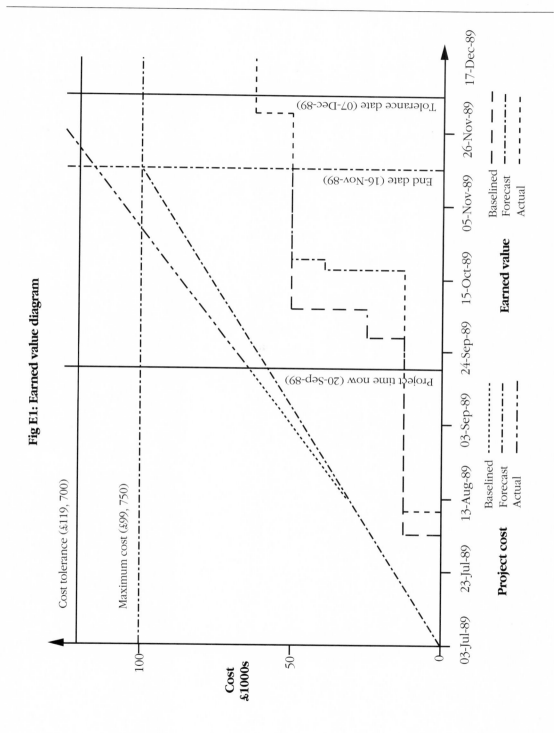

Fig E1: Earned value diagram

Bibliography

This Guide refers to the following publications.

All CCTA publications (other than the Information Systems Guides) can be obtained through: CCTA Library, Riverwalk House, 157 Millbank, London SW1 4RT

The Information Systems Guides, published by CCTA, are available from: John Wiley & Sons Ltd., Baffins Lane, Chichester PO19 1UD

Information Systems Guides:

A2: Strategic Planning for Information Systems

B1: The Users' Role in Systems Development
B2: The Feasibility study
B3: The Full Study
B4: Appraising Investment in Information Systems
B6: Procurement
B8: Systems Engineering

D1: Small Systems

E1: The Information Systems Services Industry
E2: The Hire and Management of Consultants
E3: Turnkey Projects
E4: Facilities Management

Standards:

CCTA Catalogue of Standards for Use in IT Procurements 1987 and updates.

CCTA Standards Publications

BSI 5750 - Quality Systems, Part 1 Specification for Design/Development, Production, Installation and Servicing, 1987.
British Standards Institution, 1981 & 1987.
(Also numbered ISO 9001).

ISO 9001 - see British Standards Institution BSI 5750.

Other publications:

CCTA IS Notices
(formerly known as CCTA IT Circulars).
These are temporary notices published by the CCTA; the information may later be incorporated into permanent documents.

CCTA Rules for Tendering and General Conditions of Contract - CC88

Civil Service College Prospectus 1989-90,
(published for each year).
HMSO 01

Controlling Software Projects,
DeMarco, Tom.
Yourdon Press, 1982: ISBN 0 13 171711 1 025

Ergonomic Factors Associated with the Use of Visual Display Units,
Joint Report by CCTA and Council of Civil Service Unions
CCTA May 1988.

Getting the Best out of People,
Cabinet Office & Office of the Minister for the Civil Service.
HMSO 1987: ISBN 0 11 430024 0

Guidelines for Directing Information Systems Strategy,
CCTA 1988.

Influence on Productivity of Staff Personality and Team Working,
Woodward, Chris.
PEP Paper no 7, Butler Cox & Partners Ltd, 1988.

Managing by Project Management,
Adams, John R and others.
Universal Technology Corporation, 1979.

Matrix,
Davis, S M & Paul Lawrence.
Addison-Wesley, 1977.

Planning and Managing Change,
Mayon-White, Bill.
Harper & Row and the Open University 1986: ISBN 0 06 318359 5

Principles of Software Engineering Management,
Gilb, Tom.
Addison-Wesley Publishing Co., 1988: ISBN 0 201 19246 2

Project Management - Combining Technical and Behavioural Approaches for Effective Implementation,
Graham, Robert J.
Van Nostrand Reinhold Co., New York 1985: ISBN 0 442 23018 4

Project Management - a Managerial Approach,
Meredith, Jack R & Mantel, Samuel J Jr.
John Wiley & Sons Inc 1985: ISBN 0 471 80964 0

Software Engineering Standards,
The Institute of Electrical and Electronic Engineers.
John Wiley & Sons Inc 1987: ISBN 47163457 3

System Project Management,
Yeates, Don.
Pitman Publishing Ltd., 1986: ISBN 0-273-02388-8

Methodologies

ADEPT - A Development Environment for PRINCE Tasks (Version 1.5).
Developed by Metier Management Systems Ltd for CCTA.

CRAMM - The CCTA Risk Analysis and Management Methodology.
CCTA 1988.

A Guide to CRAMM for Management.

MEVIOS - Method for Evaluating the Impact of Office Systems.
CCTA 1989.

PRINCE - Projects in Controlled Environments.
CCTA 1989.

Introduction to PRINCE
Management, Technical and Quality Guides

SSADM - Structured Systems Analysis and Design
Methodology.
NCC 1986.
Manuals available from NCC Publications.

> *Introducing SSADM - The NCC Guide: Nicholls,*
> *Derek.*
> *NCC Publications 1987: ISBN 0 85012 628 2*

Training courses

Strategic Planning for Information Systems.
Civil Service College.

Glossary

CCSU	Council of Civil Service Unions.
COMPACT	A methodology similar to SSADM, but intended for small office systems.
Configuration Item (CI)	A uniquely identifiable entity within an IT infrastructure component.
Configuration Management (CM)	A technical discipline intended to make technical and managerial activities more effective. It provides a focus for the co-ordination of activities where several different people or groups are working together.
CRAMM	CCTA Risk Analysis and Management Methodology.
End Stage Assessment (ESA)	This is a mandatory PRINCE management control. It occurs at the end of each stage. It consists of a formal presentation to the Project Board of the current project status and also requests approval of the Resource Plans and Technical Plans for the next stage. Approval by the Project Board (of the work done so far and future plans) is needed at an end stage assessment before the project can proceed (other than in a limited way) to the next stage.
Facilities Management (FM)	The provision and operation of an IT service by an external agency.
Feasibility Study	A short assessment of an information system proposed in the IS Strategy.
Full Study	An early and major component of the system development lifecycle, which analyses present systems (if any), specifies user requirements in detail, assesses ways of meeting those requirements, and produces a logical design of the proposed system.
Gantt chart	A Gantt chart shows planned activities and actual progress as horizontal bars set against a time scale. This technique was first developed by Henry L Gantt in about 1917.
GAT	General Agreement on Tariffs and Trade.

IA	Investment Appraisal.
Information System (IS)	Any procedure or process, with or without IT support, which provides a way of acquiring, storing, processing, or disseminating information. Information systems include applications and their supporting infrastructure components.
Information System lifecycle	A collective term for the various stages that an information system goes through during its existence, from its initial conception through to its final decommissioning.
IS Planning Secretariat (ISPS)	A central team providing support to the ISSC and co-ordinating the activities of the Executive Committees. The team is responsible for definition (in accordance with ISSC wishes), monitoring and review of the IS Strategy.
issue	A problem which has an effect outside the immediate environment (eg project) where it arose.
Issue Management	The management of issues. The main aims of issue management are:

- to minimise any adverse effects caused by the issue;
- to prevent the effects of the issue from spreading and affecting other work;
- to resolve the issue in the most effective and efficient way.

ISSC	See IS Steering Committee.
IS Steering Committee (ISSC)	The top management group responsible for the direction of information systems in a department. The ISSC commissions directs and agrees the IS Strategy.
ITEC	see IT Executive Committee.
IT Executive Committee (ITEC)	The senior management group responsible for the executive co-ordination, control and direction of some or all of the IT projects that result from the IS Strategy.
Matrix Management	The management of personnel from more than one work area, such as IT Directorate and one or more user divisions. This involves horizontal control across the organisational structure as well as the more usual vertical, hierarchical control.

MEVIOS	CCTA's Method for Evaluating the Impact of Office Systems.
Mid Stage Assessment (MSA)	The PRINCE Mid Stage Assessment may be held for one or more of the following reasons.

- As an interim management assessment point for the Project Board.

- To authorise limited work to begin on the next stage before the current stage is complete.

- To permit a formal Project Board review part-way through a long stage.

- To make decisions when unplanned situations arise by reviewing Exception Plans.

Operational Requirement (OR)	A document forming a step in the procurement process, containing a complete statement of the procuring department's requirements, addressed to one or more possible suppliers of equipment or services, and designed to draw from each supplier a proposal describing in detail how the supplier could meet the requirements.
OR	see Operational Requirement.
PAT	see Project Assurance Team.
PER	see Project Evaluation Report.
PERT chart	Program Evaluation and Review Technique chart, a chart used to show the interdependences of tasks within a project.
Post Implementation Review (PIR)	A formal mechanism to determine the extent to which a completed project has met its objectives and the expected benefits realised.
PRINCE	Projects in Controlled Environments, a standard methodology for project management used for IS projects in UK government departments.
Project Assurance Team (PAT)	An independent team appointed for the duration of a project to ensure that the departmental quality standards are enforced and that the end-products fulfil the project quality standards.

Project Board	The Project Board is appointed by the IT Executive Committee or possibly the IS Steering Committee, from where it derives its authority. It represents at senior management level the business, financial and technical interests of the organisation associated with a particular project. It approves, reviews and authorises the organisation, plans and resources for the project.
Project Evaluation Report (PER)	Used in the PRINCE methodology, this is a report submitted by the project board to ITEC just before the final closedown of the project. The report provides an indication of how successful the project has been in all its various aspects.
Project Initiation Document (PID)	A document created as part of the PRINCE methodology to define the Terms of Reference for the project. The PID must be approved by the Project Board at Project Initiation before the project can proceed.
project lifecycle	A collective term for the various stages a project goes through during its existence, from initiation through to final completion.
Project Manager	An individual appointed by the Project Board, and given day-to-day responsibility for producing the required products, to the required standard of quality, within specified constraints of time and cost.
PROMPT	A methodology for project management used for IS projects in UK government departments. PROMPT has now been enhanced and renamed PRINCE.
QR	Quality Review.
SSADM	Structured Systems Analysis and Design Methodology, a standard methodology for analysis and design in software development projects, developed by CCTA and used in UK government departments and in the private sector.
stage	In this guide, this refers to a stage in a project.
Stage Manager	Under PRINCE the person responsible to the Project Board for managing the stage of the project and for producing the stage end-products to the specified quality standards, on time and budget.

TAC   Technical Assurance Co-ordinator.

turnkey project   A project to provide a complete system, in which the prime
                           contractor takes full responsibility for translating the stated
                           requirement into a working system, including all necessary
                           design and installation of hardware, software and
                           documentation.

user   Any person who actually uses a system.

Index